Introduction

CW01432988

We present to you today the best.

Welcome to the world of air fryer Cakes! In this recipe book, you will discover how to make delicious, healthy, and easy-to-prepare every cakes in an air fryer.

An air fryer is an kitchen appliance that uses hot air to fry and cook food. This means that you can enjoy your favorite desserts without the added oil, making it the perfect appliance for anyone who loves to bake. So many people all over the world just fell in love with this amazing tool and now it's your turn to become one of them.

In this recipe book, you will find a wide range of sweet and indulgent desserts that can be made in your air fryer. From cakes and cupcakes to donuts and pastries, you will discover how to make classic treats with a healthier twist. Whether you are a seasoned baker or just starting out, these recipes are simple to follow and packed with flavor.

So, let's get started!
Have fun cooking with your great kitchen!

Tips for Baking with an Air Fryer

- **Preheat the air fryer:** Always preheat the fryer before adding food to ensure even cooking and best results.

- **Use nonstick cooking spray**: To prevent foods from sticking, lightly coat the basket or pan of the air fryer with nonstick cooking spray.

- **Avoid placing too much food, thick layer**: As this will prevent normal air circulation and may affect the quality of your baked goods.

- **Check your food often**: Air fryers cook food quickly, so it's important to check the food often and adjust the cooking time if necessary.

- **Use a thermometer**: To ensure that your baked goods are fully cooked, you should use a thermometer to check the internal temperature of the food.

- **Experiment**: Air fryers are versatile and can be used for a wide variety of foods, so don't be afraid to experiment with new recipes!

- The time and temperature may vary slightly depending on the make and model of the air fryer, so you **should consult the manufacturer's instructions and adjust accordingly.**

By following these tips, you will succeed in making delicious baked goods in your air fryer! I wish you success and delicious!

Table of Content

COOKIE, BISCUIT, TART

BREAD

PIE & MORE

Converting Units of Measurement In Cooking

Key Volume Conversions:

1 tablespoon = 3 teaspoons = 15 milliliters

4 tablespoons = 1/4 cup = 60 milliliters

1 ounce = 2 tablespoons = 30 milliliters

1 cup = 8 oz. = 250 milliliters

1 pint = 2 cups = 500 milliliters

1 quart = 4 cups = 950 milliliters

1 quart = 2 pints = 950 milliliters

1 gallon = 4 quarts = 3800 milliliters = 3.8 liters

Dry Ingredient Equivalents:

1 tablespoon = 3 teaspoons = 15 ml

1/8 cup = 2 tablespoons = 30 ml

1/4 cup = 4 tablespoons = 50 ml

1/3 cup = 5-1/3 tablespoons = 75 ml

1/2 cup = 8 tablespoons = 125 ml

2/3 cup = 10-2/3 tablespoons = 150 ml

3/4 cup = 12 tablespoons = 175 ml

1 cup = 16 tablespoons = 250 ml

Wet Ingredient Equivalents:

1 cup = 8 fluid ounces = 1/2 pint

2 cups = 16 fluid ounces = 1 pint

4 cups = 32 fluid ounces = 2 pints

8 cups = 64 fluid = ounces 4 pint

Chocolate Cake

🍴 Servings: 12   🕐 40 minutes

INGREDIENTS

- 1 egg.
- 1 banana, mashed.
- 3/4 cup white flour.
- 3/4 teaspoon pumpkin pie spice.
- 3/4 cup whole wheat flour.
- 1 teaspoon baking soda.
- 8 ounces canned pumpkin puree.
- 3/4 cup sugar.
- 2/3 cup chocolate chips.
- 1/2 teaspoon baking powder.
- 1/2 teaspoon vanilla extract.
- 2 tablespoons canola oil.
- 1/2 cup Greek yogurt.
- Cooking spray.

DIRECTIONS

1. Mix white flour with whole wheat flour, salt, baking soda and powder and pumpkin spice in a bowl and stir.
2. In another bowl, mix sugar with oil, banana, yogurt, pumpkin puree, vanilla and egg and stir using a mixer.
3. Combine the 2 mixtures, add chocolate chips, stir, pour this into a greased Bundt pan. (Note to choose the Bundt pan that is the right size for the air fryer)
4. Introduce in your air fryer and bake at 330 degrees F for 30 minutes.
5. Leave the cake to cool down, before cutting and serving it.

Coffee Cheesecakes

🍴 Servings: 6   🕐 30 minutes

INGREDIENTS

The cheesecakes:

- 3 eggs.
- 2 tablespoons butter.
- 1/3 cup sugar.
- 8 ounces cream cheese.
- 3 tablespoons coffee.
- 1 tablespoon caramel syrup.

The frosting:

- 3 tablespoons butter.
- 2 tablespoons sugar.
- 3 tablespoons caramel syrup.
- 8 ounces mascarpone cheese, soft.

DIRECTIONS

1. Mix cream cheese with eggs, 2 tablespoons butter, coffee, 1 tablespoon caramel syrup and 1/3 cup sugar in your blender and pulse well.
2. Pour the above mixture into a cake pan that fits in your air fryer.
3. Introduce in the fryer and bake at 320 degrees F and bake for 20 minutes.
4. Leave aside to cool down and then put it in the fridge for 3 hours.
5. Meanwhile, mix 3 tablespoons butter with 3 tablespoons caramel syrup, 2 tablespoons sugar and mascarpone in a bowl, blend well, spoon this over cheesecakes and serve them.

Lemon Pound Cake

🍴 Servings: 1 Mini Loaf   🕐 40 minutes

INGREDIENTS

- 1 large egg.
- 1 cup all-purpose flour.
- 1 teaspoon baking powder.
- 1/4 teaspoon salt.
- 1 lemon, zested.
- 6 tablespoons unsalted butter, softened.
- 1/4 cup buttermilk.
- 1/4 cup granulated sugar.
- 1 tablespoon fresh lemon juice.

Items needed: 1 mini loaf pan, greased

DIRECTIONS

1. Mix together the flour, baking powder, and salt in a bowl.
2. Beat the softened butter with an electric mixer for 3 minutes or until light and fluffy.
3. Add the sugar into the whipped butter, mix well in 1 minute.
4. Add the flour mixture into the butter mix well until fully incorporated.
5. Mix the egg, lemon juice, and lemon zest. Mix on low speed until fully incorporated. Pour in the buttermilk slowly while mixing at medium speed.
6. Add the batter to the greased mini loaf pan, filling all the way to the top.
7. Place cake into the preheated air fryer. Bake in 350 F on 35 minutes.
8. Take out and use immediately or serve cold.

Simple Cheesecake

🍴 Servings: 2   🕐 50 minutes

INGREDIENTS

- 8 ounces cream cheese softened
- 1 egg room temperature
- 0.5 teaspoon pure vanilla extract
- 3 tablespoons granulated sugar
- Graham Cracker Crust
- 5 tablespoons melted butter
- 1.5 cups crushed graham crackers
- 1/4 cup brown sugar

Simple Cheesecake
(CONTINUE)

$$\boxed{\textbf{DIRECTIONS}}$$

Make to Cracker Crust:

1. Use a food processor to grind the crackers into crumbs.
2. Combine the ingredients in a bowl and mix until the cracker are dampened and starting to stick together.
3. Line 2 mini spring form pans with parchment paper.
4. Press the crust into the bottom of each pan.
5. Bake in the air fryer at 350F degrees for 3 minutes. Remove and let cool fully (so it doesn't get soggy) before adding cheesecake filling.

Make to Cake:

1. Place the cream cheese in a bowl and beat with a mixer until slightly fluffy, about 2-3 minutes. Add the sugar and beat another 1-2 minutes. Add the egg and vanilla extract and beat for 30 seconds.
2. Pour the mixture on top of the crust and cook in the air fryer (on the air fry setting) at 300F degrees for 12 minutes.
3. Turn the air fryer off and let the cheesecake inside for 30 minutes. Remove and let cool full at room temperature.
4. Serve topped with whipped cream, strawberries, blueberries or chocolate syrup.

NOTE:

- Use full fat cream cheese for the best results.
- Having your ingredients at room temperature helps keep your filling creamy and smooth instead of lumpy.

Lime Cheesecake

🍴 Servings: 12   🕐 40 minutes

INGREDIENTS

- 2 tablespoons butter, melted.
- 1/4 cup coconut, shredded.
- 2 teaspoons sugar.
- 4 ounces flour.

The filling:
- 1 pound cream cheese.
- 2 sachets lime jelly.
- Grated Juice form 1 lime.
- Zest from 1 lime,
- 2 cups hot water.

DIRECTIONS

1. Mix coconut with flour, butter and sugar in a bowl, stir well and put this on the bottom of a pan that fits your air fryer.
2. Meanwhile, put the hot water in another bowl, add jelly sachets and stir until it dissolves.
3. Put cream cheese in a bowl, add jelly, lime juice and zest and whisk really well.
4. Add this over the crust, spread, introduce in the air fryer and cook at 300 degrees F for 4 minutes.
5. Keep in the fridge for 4 hours before servin.

Sponge Cake

🍴 Servings: 12 🕐 40 minutes

INGREDIENTS

- 1.5 cup milk.
- 1.7 cup sugar.
- 3 cups flour.
- 3 teaspoons baking powder.
- 1/2 cup cornstarch.
- 1 teaspoon baking soda.
- 1 cup olive oil.
- 1/4 cup lemon juice.
- 2 teaspoons vanilla extract.
- 2 cups water.

DIRECTIONS

1. Mix flour with cornstarch, baking powder, baking soda and sugar in a bowl and whisk well.
2. In second bowl, mix oil with milk, water, lemon juice and vanilla and whisk.
3. Combine the two mixtures, stir, pour in a greased baking dish that fits your air fryer.
4. Introduce in the fryer and bake at 350 degrees F for 20 minutes.
5. Leave cake to cool down, cut and serve.

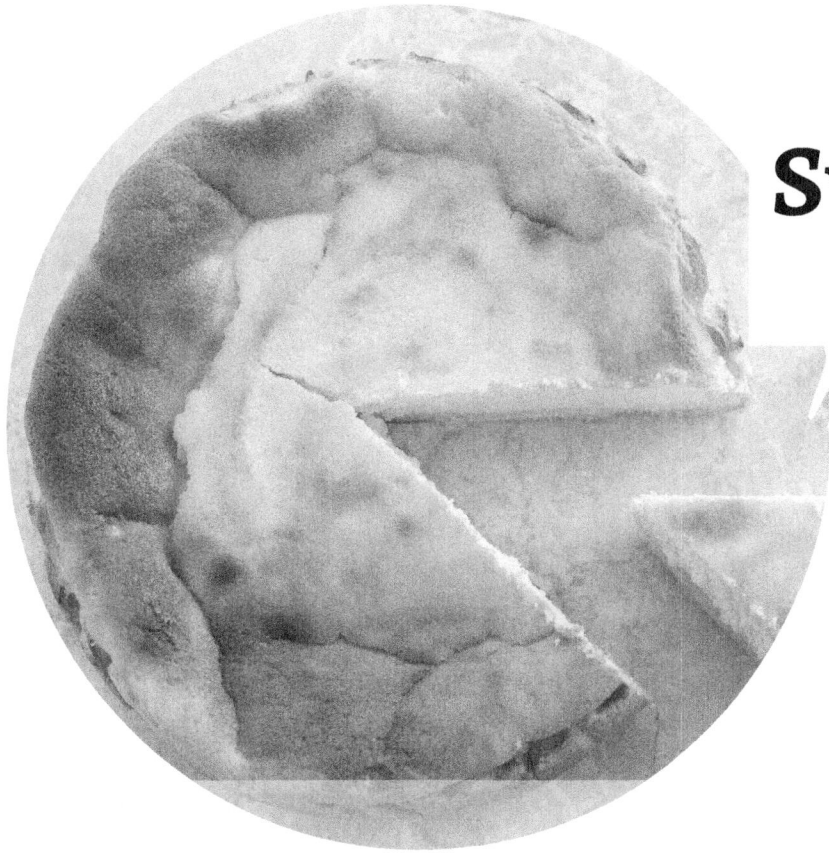

Sweet Potato Cheesecake

🍴 Servings: 4   🕐 15 minutes

INGREDIENTS

- 3/4 cup milk.
- 4 tablespoons butter, melted.
- 8 ounces cream cheese, soft.
- 6 ounces mascarpone, soft.
- 1 teaspoon vanilla extract.
- 2/3 cup graham crackers, crumbled.
- 1/4 teaspoons cinnamon powder.
- 2/3 cup sweet potato puree.

DIRECTIONS

1. Mix butter with crumbled crackers in a bowl, stir well, press on the bottom of a cake pan that fits your air fryer and keep in the fridge for now.
2. In second bowl, mix cream cheese with mascarpone, sweet potato, milk, puree, cinnamon and vanilla and whisk really well.
3. Take the pie crust out of the fridge, spread this over crust, introduce in your air fryer, cook at 300 degrees F for 5 minutes.
4. Keep in the fridge for a few hours before serving.

Carrot Cake

🍴 Servings: 6   🕐 50 minutes

INGREDIENTS

- 1 egg
- 5 ounces flour.
- ½ teaspoon cinnamon powder
- ½ teaspoon baking soda
- ¾ teaspoon baking powder
- ½ teaspoon allspice
- ¼ cup pineapple juice
- ¼ teaspoon nutmeg, ground
- 1/3 cup carrots, grated
- 3 tablespoons yogurt
- ½ cup sugar
- 1/3 cup coconut flakes, shredded
- 4 tablespoons sunflower oil
- 1/3 cup pecans, toasted and chopped
- Cooking spray.

DIRECTIONS

1. Mix flour with baking soda and powder, salt, allspice, cinnamon and nutmeg in a bowl and stir.
2. In another bowl, mix egg with yogurt, sugar, pineapple juice, oil, carrots, pecans and coconut flakes and stir well.
3. Combine the two mixtures and stir well, pour this into a spring form pan that fits your air fryer which you've greased with cooking spray,
4. Put to your air fryer and bake on 320 degrees F for 40-45 minutes.
5. Leave cake to cool down, then cut and serve it.

Cardamom Cakes

🍴 Servings: 4   🕐 15 minutes

INGREDIENTS

- 2 cups All-purpose flour.
- 1.5 cup milk.
- 1 tbsp cardamom powder.
- 1 /2 tsp baking powder.
- 1/2 tsp baking soda.
- 2 tbsp butter.
- 2 tbsp sugar.
- Muffin cups.

DIRECTIONS

1. In a bowl, mix the dry ingredients well to get a acrumbly mixture.
2. In another bowl, mix well the baking soda and the vinegar to the milk, add this milk to the mixture in step 1 and create a batter. Pour into the muffin cups.
3. Preheat the fryer to 300 F for 4 minutes. Put the muffin cups in the basket and bake for 15 minutes.
4. Remove the cups and serve hot.

INGREDIENTS

- 2 eggs, whisked.
- 3/4 cup sugar.
- 1.25 cups flour.
- 2 teaspoons lime zest, grated.
- 1 teaspoon baking powder.
- 1 tablespoon orange zest, grated.
- 1/2 cup butter, soft
- 1/2 teaspoon vanilla extract.
- 2 tablespoons poppy seeds.
- 1 cup milk.

For the cream:
- 1 cup sugar.
- 4 egg yolks.
- 3 tablespoons butter, melted.
- 1/2 cup passion fruit puree.

Poppyseed Cake

Servings: 6   40 minutes

DIRECTIONS

1. Mix flour with baking powder, 3/4 cup sugar, orange zest and lime zest in a bowl, and stir.
2. Add 1/2 cup butter, poppy seeds, eggs, vanilla and milk, stir using your mixer, pour into a cake pan that fits your air fryer and bake at 350 degrees F for about 30 minutes.
3. Meanwhile, heat up a pan with 3 tablespoons butter over medium heat, add sugar and stir until it dissolves. Add passion fruit puree and egg yolks gradually and whisk really well. Take off heat.
4. Take cake out of the fryer, cool it down a bit and cut into halves horizontally.
5. Spread 1/4 of passion fruit cream over one half, top with the other cake half and spread 1/4 of the cream on top.
6. Serve cold.

Double Funfetti Cake

🍴 Servings: 6   🕐 40 minutes

- 2 large eggs.
- 2 teaspoons vanilla extract.
- 1 cup granulated sugar.
- 1.5 cups all-purpose flour.
- 1.5 teaspoons baking powder.
- 1/4 teaspoon salt.
- 1/2 cup unsalted butter, at room temperature.
- 1/2 cup whole milk.
- 1/2 cup rainbow sprinkles.
- Additional rainbow sprinkles for decorating.

DIRECTIONS

1. In a mixing bowl, whisk together the flour, baking powder, and salt.
2. In a large bowl, using an electric mixer, cream together the butter and sugar until light and fluffy. Add the eggs one at a time, beating well after each addition. Mix in the vanilla extract.
3. Gradually add the flour mixture to the butter mixture, alternating with the milk, and mix until just combined. Stir in the 1/2 cup of sprinkles.
4. Preheat your air fryer to 320°F for 5 minutes. Pour the batter into a greased 7-inch cake pan that fits in your air fryer. Sprinkle additional rainbow sprinkles on top of the cake.
5. Put the cake pan in the air fryer basket and cook for 25-30 minutes, or until a toothpick inserted into the center of the cake comes out clean.
6. Let the cake cool in the pan for 10 minutes before removing it to a wire rack to cool completely.
7. Serve and enjoy!

For the cake:

- 1 large egg.
- 1/2 cup unsalted butter, softened.
- 3/4 cup granulated sugar.
- 1/2 teaspoon vanilla extract.
- 1.5 cups all-purpose flour.
- 1/2 teaspoon baking powder.
- 1/4 teaspoon salt.
- 1/2 cup whole milk.
- 1.5 cups fresh blueberries.

For the crumble topping:

- 1/2 cup all-purpose flour.
- 1/4 cup unsalted butter, chilled and cut into small cubes.
- 1/4 cup granulated sugar.
- 1/4 teaspoon ground cinnamon.

Blueberry Shortbread Crumble Cake

Servings: 6   40 minutes

DIRECTIONS

1. In a large bowl, using an electric mixer, cream together the butter and sugar until light and fluffy. Add the egg and vanilla extract, and mix until well combined.

2. In a separate bowl, whisk together the flour, baking powder, and salt.

3. Gradually add the flour mixture to the butter mixture, alternating with the milk, and mix until just combined. Fold in the blueberries.

4. Preheat your air fryer to 320°F for 5 minutes. Pour the batter into a greased 7-inch cake pan that fits in your air fryer.

5. In a separate bowl, combine the flour, chilled butter cubes, sugar, and cinnamon. Use your fingers to rub the ingredients together until the mixture resembles coarse breadcrumbs. Sprinkle the crumble topping evenly over the cake batter.

6. Put the cake pan in the air fryer basket and bake for 25-30 minutes, or until a toothpick inserted into the center of the cake comes out clean.

7. Let the cake cool in the pan for 10 minutes before removing it to a wire rack to cool completely. Serve and enjoy!

Coconut Macadamia White Chocolate Cake

🍴 Servings: 8   🕐 45 minutes

INGREDIENTS

For the cake:

- 2 large eggs.
- 1/4 teaspoon salt.
- 1/2 cup whole milk.
- 1/2 cup unsalted butter, softened.
- 3/4 cup granulated sugar.
- 1/2 teaspoon vanilla extract.
- 1.5 cups all-purpose flour.
- 1/2 teaspoon baking powder.
- 1/2 cup sweetened shredded coconut.
- 1/2 cup chopped macadamia nuts.
- 1/2 cup white chocolate chips.

For the glaze:

- 1/2 cup white chocolate chips.
- 2 tablespoons unsalted butter.
- 2 tablespoons heavy cream.
- 1/2 teaspoon vanilla extract.

DIRECTIONS

1. Using an electric mixer, cream together the butter and sugar until light and fluffy. Add the eggs and vanilla extract, and mix until well combined.
2. In a separate bowl, whisk together the flour, baking powder, and salt.
3. Gradually add the flour mixture to the butter mixture, alternating with the milk, and mix until just combined. Fold in the shredded coconut, chopped macadamia nuts, and white chocolate chips.
4. Preheat your air fryer to 320°F for 5 minutes. Pour the batter into a greased cake pan that fits in your air fryer. Place the cake pan in the air fryer basket and cook for 25-30 minutes, or until a toothpick inserted into the center of the cake comes out clean.
5. Let the cake cool in the pan for 10 minutes before removing it to a wire rack to cool completely.
6. In a microwave-safe bowl, heat the white chocolate chips, butter, and heavy cream in 20-second intervals, stirring after each interval, until melted and smooth. Stir in the vanilla extract. Drizzle the glaze over the cooled cake. Serve!

Passion Fruit Coconut Cake

🍴 Servings: 4   🕐 45 minutes

For the cake:
- 2 large eggs.
- 1/2 cup unsalted butter, softened.
- 1 cup granulated sugar.
- 1/2 teaspoon vanilla extract.
- 1.5 cups all-purpose flour.
- 1 teaspoon baking powder.
- 1/4 teaspoon salt.
- 1/2 cup whole milk.
- 1/2 cup sweetened shredded coconut..
- 1/4 cup passion fruit puree.

For the glaze:
- 1 cup powdered sugar.
- 2 tablespoons passion fruit puree.
- 1/4 cup sweetened shredded coconut, toasted.

DIRECTIONS

1. Using an electric mixer, cream together the butter and sugar until light and fluffy. Add the eggs and vanilla extract, and mix until well combined.
2. In a separate bowl, whisk together the flour, baking powder, and salt. Gradually add the flour mixture to the butter mixture, alternating with the milk, and mix until just combined. Fold in the shredded coconut and passion fruit puree.
3. Preheat your air fryer to 320°F for 5 minutes. Pour the batter into a greased cake pan that fits in your air fryer.
4. Place the cake pan in the air fryer basket and bake for 25-30 minutes, or until a toothpick inserted into the center of the cake comes out clean. Let the cake cool in the pan before removing it to a wire rack to cool completely.
5. In a small bowl, whisk together the powdered sugar and passion fruit puree until smooth. Drizzle the glaze over the cooled cake. Sprinkle the toasted shredded coconut over the top of the glaze. Serve and enjoy!

For the cake:

- 2 large eggs.
- 1 cup granulated sugar.
- 1 teaspoon vanilla extract.
- 1 teaspoon baking powder.
- 1.5 cups all-purpose flour.
- 1/2 cup unsalted butter, softened.
- 1/4 teaspoon salt.
- 1/2 cup whole milk.
- 1/2 cup cherry pie filling.

For the topping:

- 1/2 cup all-purpose flour.
- 1/2 cup rolled oats.
- 1/2 cup packed brown sugar.
- 1/2 cup unsalted butter, melted.
- 1/2 cup chopped pecans.

Cherry Pie Cake

Servings: 6   40 minutes

DIRECTIONS

1. In a large bowl, using an electric mixer, cream together the butter and sugar until light and fluffy. Add the eggs and vanilla extract, and mix until well combined.

2. In a separate bowl, whisk together the flour, baking powder, and salt. Gradually add the flour mixture to the butter mixture, alternating with the milk, and mix until just combined. Fold in the cherry pie filling.

3. In a separate bowl, mix together the flour, rolled oats, brown sugar, melted butter, and chopped pecans until crumbly. Sprinkle the topping over the cake batter.

4. Preheat your air fryer to 320°F for 5 minutes. Pour the batter into a greased cake pan that fits in your air fryer. Place the cake pan in the air fryer basket and bake for 25-30 minutes, or until a toothpick inserted into the center of the cake comes out clean.

5. Let the cake cool in the pan before removing it to a wire rack to cool completely. Serve and enjoy!

Rose Water Cake

🍴 Servings: 6   🕐 40 minutes

INGREDIENTS

For the cake:
- 2 large eggs.
- 1 tablespoon rose water.
- 1/2 cup unsalted butter, softened
- 1 cup granulated sugar
- 1 teaspoon vanilla extract.
- 1 teaspoon baking powder.
- 1.5 cups all-purpose flour.
- 1/4 teaspoon salt.
- 1/2 cup whole milk.

For the frosting:
- 1/2 cup unsalted butter, softened.
- 2 cups powdered sugar.
- 2 tablespoons whole milk.
- 1 tablespoon rose water.
- Pink food coloring (optional).

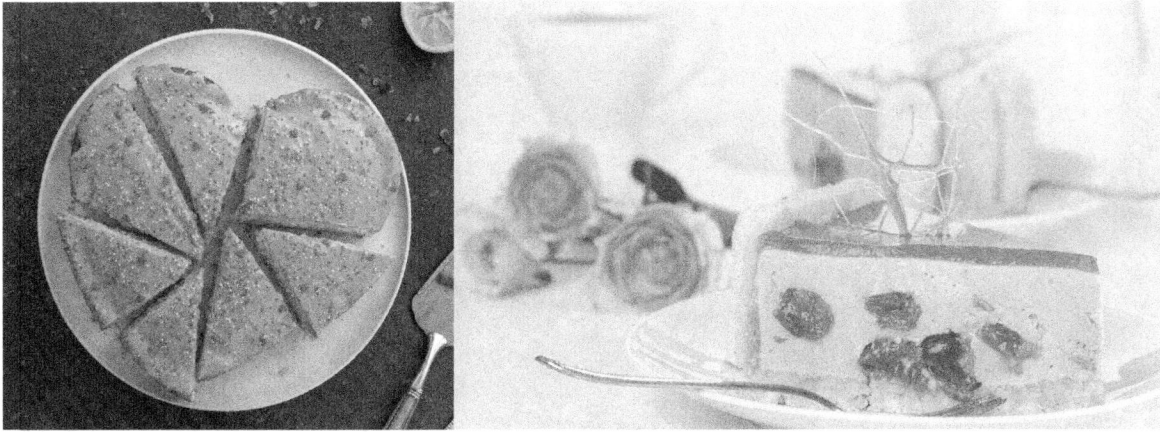

DIRECTIONS MAKE ROSE WATER CAKE

1. In a large bowl, using an electric mixer, cream together the butter and sugar until light and fluffy. Add the eggs and vanilla extract, and mix until well combined.

2. In a separate bowl, whisk together the flour, baking powder, and salt. Gradually add the flour mixture to the butter mixture, alternating with the milk and rose water, and mix until just combined.

3. Preheat your air fryer to 320°F for 5 minutes. Pour the batter into a greased cake pan that fits in your air fryer.

4. Place the cake pan in the air fryer basket and bake for 25-30 minutes, or until a toothpick inserted into the center of the cake comes out clean. Let the cake cool in the pan before removing it to a wire rack to cool completely.

5. To make the frosting, using an electric mixer, cream together the butter and powdered sugar until light and fluffy.

6. Gradually add the milk and rose water, and mix until the frosting is smooth and spreadable.(If desired, add a few drops of pink food coloring to the frosting and mix until you reach your desired shade of pink)

7. Once the cake has cooled completely, use a long, serrated knife to level off the top of the cake. Spread the frosting over the top of the cake. Serve and enjoy!

Note: If you don't have rose water, you can substitute it with another flavor extract, such as vanilla or almond.

Cannoli Cake

🍴 Servings: 6   🕐 40 minutes

INGREDIENTS

For the cake:
- 2 large eggs.
- 1.5 cups all-purpose flour.
- 1/2 cup unsalted butter, softened.
- 1 cup granulated sugar.
- 1 teaspoon vanilla extract.
- 1 teaspoon baking powder.
- 1/4 teaspoon salt.
- 1/2 cup whole milk.

For the filling:
- 1 cup ricotta cheese.
- 1/2 cup powdered sugar.
- 1/4 cup mini chocolate chips.
- 1/4 cup chopped pistachios.

For the frosting:
- 1/2 cup unsalted butter, softened
- 2 cups powdered sugar
- 2 tablespoons whole milk
- 1/2 teaspoon vanilla extract.

DIRECTIONS MAKE CANNOLI CAKE

1. Using an electric mixer, cream together the butter and sugar until light and fluffy. Add the eggs and vanilla extract, and mix until well combined.
2. In a separate bowl, whisk together the flour, baking powder, and salt. Gradually add the flour mixture to the butter mixture, alternating with the milk, and mix until just combined.
3. Preheat your air fryer to 320°F for 5 minutes. Pour the batter into a greased cake pan that fits in your air fryer.
4. Place the cake pan in the air fryer basket and bake for 25-30 minutes, or until a toothpick inserted into the center of the cake comes out clean.
5. Let the cake cool in the pan before removing it to a wire rack to cool completely.
6. In a separate bowl, mix together the ricotta cheese and powdered sugar until smooth. Fold in the mini chocolate chips and chopped pistachios.
7. To make the frosting, using an electric mixer, cream together the butter and powdered sugar until light and fluffy. Gradually add the milk and vanilla extract, and mix until the frosting is smooth and spreadable.
8. Once the cake has cooled completely, use a long, serrated knife to level off the top of the cake. Spread the ricotta filling on top of the cake. Spread the frosting over the ricotta filling. Sprinkle additional chopped pistachios and mini chocolate chips over the top of the frosting. Serve.

Ricotta and Lemon Cake

🍴 Servings: 4   🕐 1 hour and 10 minutes

INGREDIENTS

- 8 eggs, whisked.
- 1/2 pound sugar.
- 3 pounds ricotta cheese.
- Zest from 1 orange.
- Zest from 1 lemon, grated.
- Grated Butter for the pan.

DIRECTIONS

1. Mix eggs with sugar, cheese, lemon and orange zest in a bowl, and stir very well.
2. Grease a baking pan that fits your air fryer with some batter, spread ricotta mixture.
3. Put in the fryer at 390 degrees F and bake for 30 minutes.
4. Reduce heat at 380 degrees F and bake for 40 more minutes.
5. Take out of the oven, leave cake to cool down and serve!

Stuffed French Toast

🍴 Servings: 1   🕐 15 minutes

INGREDIENTS

- 2 eggs.
- 1 Slice brioche bread, 2.5 inches thick, preferably stale.
- 4 ounces cream cheese.
- 1 teaspoon cinnamon.
- 2 tablespoons milk.
- 2 tablespoons heavy cream.
- 3 tablespoons sugar.
- 1/2 teaspoon vanilla extract.
- Pistachios, chopped, for topping.
- Maple syrup, for serving.
- Cooking spray.

DIRECTIONS

1. Cut a slit in the middle of the brioche slice, stuff the inside of the slit with cream cheese. Set aside.
2. Whisk together the eggs, milk, heavy cream, sugar, cinnamon, and vanilla extract in a bowl.
3. Soak the stuffed French toast in the egg mixture for 10 seconds on each side. Then Spray each side of the French toast with cooking spray.
4. Place the French toast into the preheated air fryer. Bake in 10 minutes on 350°F .
5. Remove the French toast carefully when done cooking.
6. Top with chopped pistachios and serve with maple syrup.

Stuffed Cinnamon Toast

🍴 Servings: 2   🕐 20 minutes

INGREDIENTS

- 2 eggs.
- 1 Slice brioche bread, 2.5 inches thick, preferably stale.
- 4 ounces cream cheese.
- 1 teaspoon cinnamon.
- 2 tablespoons milk.
- 2 tablespoons heavy cream.
- 3 tablespoons sugar.
- 1/2 teaspoon vanilla extract.
- Pistachios, chopped, for topping.
- Maple syrup, for serving.
- Cooking spray.

DIRECTIONS

1. Cut a slit in the middle of the brioche slice, stuff the inside of the slit with cream cheese. Set aside.
2. Whisk together the eggs, milk, heavy cream, sugar, cinnamon, and vanilla extract in a bowl.
3. Soak the stuffed French toast in the egg mixture for 10 seconds on each side. Then Spray each side of the French toast with cooking spray.
4. Place the French toast into the preheated air fryer. Bake in 10 minutes on 350°F .
5. Remove the French toast carefully when done cooking.
6. Top with chopped pistachios and serve with maple syrup.

Simple Pancakes

🍴 Servings: 14   🕐 15 minutes

INGREDIENTS

- 120g Pancake Mix of your choice.
- 60g Whey/Casein Blend Vanilla Protein Powder.
- 30g PB Party Protein Cookie Butter Powder.
- 24g Coconut Flour.
- 8g Zero Cal Sweetener of your choice.
- 8g Baking Powder.
- 150g Egg Whites.
- Unsweetened Vanilla.
- Almond Milk to the consistency of batter.

DIRECTIONS

1. Mix all of your dry ingredients in a bowl to avoid clumping, then add in your wet ingredients and mix some more. Add in a little bit of almond milk at a time and mix, then repeat until you reach a batter-like consistency.
2. Add 1/14th of your batter to the pan. Place a cover on top and cook your pancakes until you see little air bubbles coming from the top of the pancakes, then flip them over.
3. Bake the pancakes on that side for another 2 minutes and repeat this process until all 14 pancakes are cooked.

TIP: If you want to store it in the fridge, Once they're cool, put them in a Ziplock bag and suck all the air out of the bag , then put them in your freezer. To reheat them, use either your toaster or air fryer!

Pumpkin Pancakes

🍴 Servings: 12   🕐 15 minutes

INGREDIENTS

- 3 eggs.
- 1 large pumpkin (shredded).
- 2 tsp dried basil.
- 1.5 cups almond flour.
- 2 tsp dried parsley.
- Salt and Pepper to taste.
- 3 tbsp Butter.

DIRECTIONS

1. Mix well the ingredients together in a bowl until the mixture is smooth and well balanced.
2. Take a pancake mold and grease it with butter. Add the batter to the mold and place it in preheated air fryer basket. Bake in 320 F for 5 mins or till both the sides of the pancake have browned on both sides and serve with maple syrup.

Honey & Orange Pancakes

Servings: 16   18 minutes

INGREDIENTS

- 3 eggs.
- 1 orange (zested).
- 3 tbsp Butter.
- 1.5 cups almond flour.
- 2 tsp dried parsley.
- 1 tbsp honey.
- 2 tsp dried basil.
- Salt and Pepper to taste.

DIRECTIONS

1. Mix well the ingredients together in a bowl until the mixture is smooth and well balanced.
2. Take a pancake mold and grease it with butter. Add the batter to the mold and place it in preheated air fryer basket. Bake in 320 F for 5 mins or till both the sides of the pancake have browned on both sides and serve with maple syrup.

Tangerine Cake

🍴 Servings: 8   🕐 20 minutes

INGREDIENTS

- 1/2 cup milk.
- 3/4 cup sugar.
- 1/2 teaspoon vanilla extract.
- 2 cups flour.
- 1/4 cup olive oil.
- 1 teaspoon cider vinegar.
- Juice and zest from 1 tangerine.
- Juice and zest from 2 lemons.
- Tangerine segments, for serving.

DIRECTIONS

1. Mix flour with sugar in a bowl and stir.
2. In second bowl, mix oil with milk, vanilla extract, vinegar, lemon juice and zest and tangerine zest and whisk very well.
3. Combine the 2 mixtures in 2 bowls together, stir well, pour this into a cake pan that fits your air fryer, introduce in the fryer and cook at 360 degrees F for 20 minutes.
4. Serve right away with tangerine segments on top.

Orange Cake

🍴 Servings: 12 🕐 40 minutes

INGREDIENTS

- 1 teaspoon baking powder.
- 6 eggs.
- 4 ounces yogur.
- 1 orange, peeled and cut into quarters.
- 1 teaspoon vanilla extract.
- 9 ounces flour.
- 2 ounces + 2 tablespoons sugar.
- 2 tablespoons orange zest.
- 4 ounces cream cheese.

DIRECTIONS

1. Puree oranges in a food processor.
2. Add flour, 2 tablespoons sugar, eggs, baking powder, vanilla extract and pulse well again.
3. Pour the above mixture into the baking pan. then put in an air fryer and bake at 330 degrees F for 16 minutes.
4. Meanwhile, mix cream cheese with orange zest, yogurt and the rest of the sugar in a bowl and stir well.
5. Place one cake layer on a plate, add half of the cream cheese mix, add the other cake layer and top with the rest of the cream cheese mix.
6. Spread it well, slice and serve.

Triple Berry Turnovers

🍴 Servings: 6   🕐 40 minutes

INGREDIENTS

- 1/2 cup mixed berries, chopped.
- 1/2 cup berry jam.
- 1 pkg (14 oz) refrigerator rolled pie pastry.
- 1 egg.
- 1/2 cup icing sugar.
- 1 tbsp milk.

DIRECTIONS

1. Mix together berries and jam. Let stand for 8 minutes.
2. On lightly floured surface, roll out pie pastry; using 5-inch ring mold or round cookie cutter, cut out 6 rounds.
3. Whisk egg with 2 tsp water; brush over one-half of the edges of pastry rounds. Spread 1 tbsp berry jam over egg-washed half of pastry rounds, leaving border; fold remaining pastry over jam and press edges firmly with fork to seal. Pierce top of tarts with fork to make steam vents. Warm up remaining berry jam.
4. Brush top of tarts with remaining egg wash. Place tarts in bowl of air-fryer. Bake at 300 F in 12 - 15 minutes or until golden and flaky. Let cool completely.
5. Stir icing sugar with milk until smooth. Drizzle turnovers with icing and top with remaining berry jam.

Tip: Try peaches and peach jam, apples and apple butter or cherries and cherry jam.

Strawberry Cream Cake

🍴 Servings: 12 🕐 25 minutes

INGREDIENTS

- 2 cups all-purpose flour.
- 1/4 cup granulated sugar.
- 2 teaspoons baking powder.
- 1/4 teaspoon salt.
- 6 tablespoons butter, cold, cut into pieces.
- 1/2 cup fresh strawberries, chopped.
- 1/2 cup heavy cream, cold.
- 2 large eggs.
- 2 teaspoons vanilla extract.
- 1 teaspoon water.
- Granulated sugar, for topping.

Items needed: 1 round 2.5 inch cookie cutter

DIRECTIONS

1. Sift together the flour, sugar, baking powder, and salt in a large bowl. Then cut the butter into the flour until the mixture resembles coarse crumbs.
2. Mix the strawberries into the flour mixture. Set aside.
3. In another bowl, whisk together the heavy cream, 1 egg, and the vanilla extract.
4. Fold the cream mixture into the flour mixture until combined, then roll it out to a 1½-inch thickness.
5. Use the 2.5-inch round cookie cutter to cut the scones.
6. Dip the scones in the mixture made from 1 egg and stirred water, Sprinkle with granulated sugar.
7. Line baking paper in the preheated air fryer basket. Then place the scones on top of paper.
8. Set time to 12 minutes in 330 °F.
9. Remove when golden brown and serve.

Strawberry Cupcakes

INGREDIENTS

- 100g Butter.
- 100g Caster Sugar.
- 2 Medium Eggs.
- 100g Self Raising Flour .
- 1/2 Tsp Vanilla Essence.
- 50g Butter.
- 100g Icing Sugar.
- 1/2 Tsp Pink Food Colouring.
- 1 Tbsp Whipped Cream.
- 1/4 Cup Fresh.
- Strawberries (blended)

Servings: 10   25 minutes

DIRECTIONS

1. Mix cream the butter and sugar in a large mixing bowl until the mixture is light and fluffy.
2. Add the vanilla essence and beat in the eggs one at a time. After adding each egg add a little of the flour. Gently fold in the rest of the flour.
3. Put them to little bun cases so that they are 1/3. Then put them in a preheated air fryer for 5 minutes and then bake for 8 minutes at 170 degrees Celsius.
4. While the cupcakes are cooking make the topping. Cream the butter and gradually add the icing sugar until you have a creamy mixture. Add the food colouring, whipped cream and blended strawberries and mix well
5. Once the cupcakes are cooked, using a piping bag add your topping to them doing circular motions so that you have that lovely cupcake look and serve.

Strawberry Shortcakes

🍴 Servings: 6 🕐 45 minutes

INGREDIENTS

- 1 cup buttermilk.
- 1/3 cup butter.
- 1/4 cup+ 4 tablespoons sugar.
- 1.5 cup flour.
- 1 tablespoon mint, chopped.
- 1 teaspoon baking powder.
- 1/4 teaspoon baking soda.
- 1 egg, whisked.
- 2 cups strawberries, sliced.
- 1 tablespoon rum.
- 1 teaspoon lime zest, grated.
- 1/2 cup whipping cream.
- Cooking spray.

DIRECTIONS

1. Mix flour with 1/2 cup sugar, baking powder and baking soda in a bowl and stir.
2. In second bowl, mix buttermilk with egg, stir, add flour mixture in step 1 and whisk.
3. Scoop this dough into 6 jars greased with cooking spray, cover with tin foil, arrange them in your air fryer bake at 360 degrees F for 45 minutes.
4. Meanwhile, in third bowl, mix strawberries with 3 tablespoons sugar, rum, mint and lime zest, stir and leave aside in a cold place.
5. In another bowl, mix whipping cream with 1 tablespoon sugar and stir.
6. Take jars out, divide strawberry mix and whipped cream on top and serve.

Mini Chocolate Peanut Butter Cupcakes

🍴 Servings: 40   🕐 45 minutes

INGREDIENTS

- 1 cup peanut butter.
- 1/4 cup water, boiling.
- Peanut Butter Frosting.
- 1 stick unsalted butter, softened.
- 2 cups confectioners sugar.
- 1 tbsp whole milk
- Garnish
- Chocolate pearls

- 1 large egg.
- 1/2 cup whole milk.
- 1 cup sugar.
- 1 tsp baking powder.
- 1/4 cup vegetable oil.
- 1.5 tsp vanilla extract.
- 2/3 cup flour.
- 1/3 cup cocoa.
- 1/2 tsp baking soda.
- 1/2 tsp salt.

DIRECTIONS

1. Mix the egg, 1/2 cup milk, vegetable oil, and vanilla in a bowl and whisk to combine.
2. Combine the flour, sugar, cocoa, baking powder, baking soda, and salt with the egg mixture and stir.
3. Slowly add the boiling water to the mixture and whisk the mixture well.
4. Pour the batter into mini aluminum cupcake liners until about two-thirds of each cupcake liner is filled.
5. Place the cake pans in the preheated air fryer. Bake on 15-min in 350° F.
6. In that time, combine the peanut butter and the butter in a bowl. Add the confectioners' sugar and 1 tbsp. milk slowly until the frosting is creamy.
7. Let the cupcakes cool for 30 mins.
8. Top the cupcakes with the frosting and the chocolate pearls and serve.

Maple Cupcakes

🍴 Servings: 4   🕐 30 minutes

INGREDIENTS

- 4 eggs.
- 4 tablespoons butter.
- 2 teaspoons cinnamon powder.
- 1/2 cup pure applesauce.
- 1/2 apple, cored and chopped.
- 1 teaspoon vanilla extract.
- 3/4 cup white flour.
- 4 teaspoons maple syrup.
- 1/2 teaspoon baking powder.

DIRECTIONS

1. Heat up a pan with the butter over medium heat, add applesauce, vanilla, eggs and maple syrup, stir, take off heat and leave aside to cool down.
2. Add flour, cinnamon, baking powder and apples, whisk.
3. Pour in a cupcake pan, introduce in your air fryer at 360 degrees F and bake for 20 minutes.
4. Leave cupcakes them to cool down, transfer to a platter and serve them.

Pumpkin Cupcakes

🍴 Servings: 12 🕐 30 minutes

INGREDIENTS

- 2 large eggs.
- 1 cup all-purpose flour.
- 2 teaspoons pumpkin pie spice.
- 1/2 teaspoon baking powder.
- 1/2 cup sugar.
- 1/4 teaspoon kosher salt.
- 1 stick unsalted butter, room temperature.
- 1/2 cup pumpkin puree.
- 1.5 teaspoon vanilla extract.

DIRECTIONS

1. Sift together the flour, pie spice, baking powder and salt, set aside.
2. With a hand or stand mixer, cream the sugar and butter together until light and fluffy, about 3-4 minutes. Add the pumpkin puree, vanilla and eggs, and mix until smooth and creamy. Slowly add the dry ingredients, mixing until incorporated.
3. Line each silicone muffin cup with a parchment cupcake liner. Fill each cupcake liner 2/3 of the way.
4. Put the cake cups in the air fryer basket. Set temperature to 350 F degrees in 12 minutes.
5. To check for doneness, insert a toothpick in the center of one cupcake. If it comes out clean, it is cooked through.
6. Remove cupcakes to a rack to cool and serve. Cover with Maple Cream Cheese Icing, and sprinkle with brown sugar, if desired.

Black Tea Cake

🍴 Servings: 12 🕐 40 minutes

INGREDIENTS

- 6 tablespoons black tea powder.
- 2 cups milk.
- 1/2 cup butter.
- 2 cups sugar.
- 4 eggs.
- 2 teaspoons vanilla extract.
- 1/2 cup olive oil.
- 3.5 cups flour.
- 1 teaspoon baking soda.
- 3 teaspoons baking powder

For the cream:
- 6 tablespoons honey.
- 4 cups sugar.
- 1 cup butter, soft.

DIRECTIONS

1. Put the milk in a pot, heat up over low heat, add tea, stir well, take off heat and leave aside to cool down.
2. Mix 1/2 cup butter with 2 cups sugar, eggs, vegetable oil, vanilla extract, baking powder, baking soda and 3.5 cups flour in a bowl and stir everything really well.
3. Pour this mixture into 2 greased round pans, introduce each in the fryer at 330 degrees F and bake for 25 minutes.
4. Mix 1 cup butter with honey and 4 cups sugar in another bowl and stir really well.
5. Arrange one cake on a platter, spread the cream all over, top with the other cake and keep in the fridge until you serve it.

Plum Cake

🍴 Servings: 8   🕐 40 minutes

INGREDIENTS

- 1 egg, whisked.
- 7 ounces flour.
- 1 ounce butter, soft.
- 1 package dried yeast.
- 5 tablespoons sugar.
- 1.3 pounds plums, pitted and cut into quarters.
- 3 ounces warm milk.
- Zest from 1 lemon, grated
- 1 ounce almond flakes.

DIRECTIONS

1. Mix yeast with butter, flour and 3 tablespoons sugar in a bowl and stir well.
2. Add milk and egg and whisk for 4 minutes until your obtain a dough.
3. Arrange the dough in a spring form pan greased with some butter, put them your air fryer and which you've , cover and leave aside for 1 hour.
4. Arrange plumps on top of the butter, sprinkle the rest of the sugar, introduce in your air fryer at 350 degrees F, bake for 35 minutes.
5. Cool down, sprinkle almond flakes and lemon zest on top, slice and serve.

Cranberry Cakes

🍴 Servings: 4   🕐 25 minutes

INGREDIENTS

- 1.5 cup milk.
- 2 cups All-purpose flour.
- 2 tbsp butter.
- 1/2 tsp baking powder.
- 1 /2 tsp baking soda.
- 2 tsp vinegar.
- 2 tbsp sugar.
- 2 cups grated cranberries Muffin cups

DIRECTIONS

1. Mix well flour, sugar, butter, baking powder and grated cranberries together until to get acrumbly mixture.
2. Add the baking soda and the vinegar to the milk and mix continuously. Add this milk to the mixture in step 1 and create a batter, which you will need to transfer to the muffin cups.
3. Preheat the fryer to 330 F for 4 minutes. You will need to place the muffin cups in the basket and cover it. Bake the muffins for 15 minutes and check whether or not the muffins are cooked using a toothpick.
4. Remove the cups and serve hot.

Chocolate Sponge Cake

🍴 Servings: 8   🕐 20 minutes

INGREDIENTS

- 1/2 cup condensed milk.
- 1 cup all-purpose flour.
- 1/2 cup cocoa powder.
- 1/2 tsp baking soda.
- 1/2 tsp baking powder.
- 1/2 cup oil.
- 3 tbsp powdered sugar,
- 1/2 cup soda.
- 1 tsp vanilla essence.
- Parchment or butter paper to line the tin

DIRECTIONS

1. Mix well the ingredients together to create a batter that is smooth and thick.
2. Grease the cake tin with butter and line the bottom with paper. Pour the mixture from step 1 into the cake tin and place it in the preheated air fryer basket.
3. Bake the cake for 15 minutes in 350 F and check whether or not the cake is cooked using a toothpick.
4. Remove the tin and cut the cake into slices and serve.

Chocolate Muffins

🍴 Servings: 12   🕐 25 minutes

INGREDIENTS

- 2 Medium Eggs
- 100g Butter
- 200g Self Raising
- 225 Caster Sugar
- 1/2 Tsp Vanilla Essence
- 25g Cocoa Powder
- 75g Milk Chocolate
- 5 Tbsp Milk Water

DIRECTIONS

1. Mix the flour, sugar and cocoa in a large mixing bowl. Rub in the butter until have a breadcrumbs consistency.

2. In second bowl, crack the eggs, add the milk and mix well. Add the egg/milk mixture into the large mixing bowl and mix well.

3. Add the vanilla essence, mix well and then add a little water if it is too thick. You have something that resembles a bun mix.

4. Using a rolling pin bash your milk chocolate in a sandwich bag until they are a mix of sizes. Add it to the bowl and mix again for the last time.

5. Spoon into little bun cases and put the muffins into the preheated air fryer. Bake for 9 minutes on 180c followed by 6 minutes on 160c. And serve.

Blueberry Muffins

Servings: 6   45 minutes

INGREDIENTS

- 275g Egg Whites.
- 75g Whey/Casein Blend Vanilla Protein Powder.
- 100g Frozen Blueberries
- 30g Blueberry Pastry Protein Cookie Butter Powder.
- 30g All Purpose Flour.
- 10g Baking Powder.
- 20g Coconut Flour.
- 10g Zero Cal Sweetener of your choice.
- 275g Plain Nonfat Greek Yogurt.
- 100g Unsweetened Apple Sauce.

DIRECTIONS

1. Mix well all the dry ingredients together in a bowl to avoid clumping, then add in your wet ingredients and mix some more. Don't any chunks or clumps. When everything's mixed together, let the batter sit for 15-20 minutes to thicken up.

2. Mix frozen blueberries with the batter, then spray silicon jump muffin molds with nonstick cooking spray. Evenly pour the batter into 6 molds. Be sure to leave enough space between them get don't oddly shaped muffins.

3. Baking the muffins at 250 degrees F for 32-35 minutes. When done, let them cool in their molds for 10-15 minutes, then serve.

Blueberry Lemon Muffins

🍴 Servings: 8   🕐 25 minutes

INGREDIENTS

- 1 cup all-purpose flour.
- 1/2 teaspoon lemon juice.
- 1/4 teaspoon baking soda.
- 1/2 cup coconut milk or soy milk.
- 1 lemon, zested.
- 1 teaspoon baking powder.
- 1/4 cup granulated sugar.
- 1/4 teaspoon salt.
- 1 cup fresh blueberries.
- 3 tablespoons liquidated coconut oil.
- 1/2 teaspoon vanilla extract.
- Cooking spray.

Items needed: 1 (6-cup) muffin pan or baking cups.

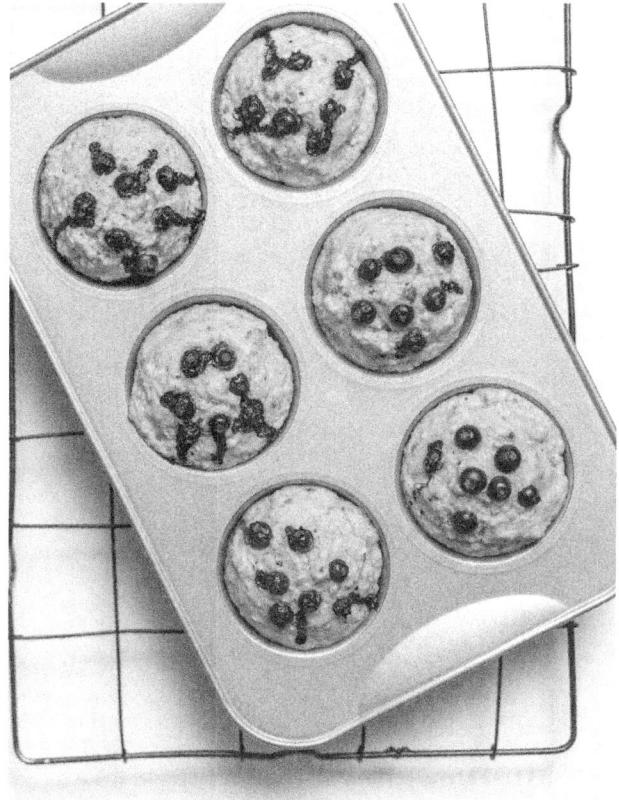

DIRECTIONS

1. Mix lemon juice and coconut/soy milk in a small bowl, then set aside. Mix together flour, baking powder, baking soda, and salt in a separate bowl.
2. Blend sugar, coconut oil, lemon zest, and vanilla extract in third bowl. Combine with lemon-milk mixture in step 1 and stir.
3. Mix the dry mixture into the wet gradually, until smooth. Gently fold in blueberries.
4. Grease muffin cups with cooking spray and pour in batter until cups are ¾ full. Put the muffins carefully into the preheated air fryer. Bake for 300°F in 15 minutes.
5. Remove muffins when done cooking, let cool then serve.

Chocolate Chip Muffins

🍴 Servings: 8   🕐 25 minutes

INGREDIENTS

- 1 cup all-purpose flour
- 1/4 cup granulated sugar.
- 1/2 teaspoon vanilla extract.
- 1/2 cup coconut milk or soy milk.
- 3 tablespoons liquidated coconut oil.
- 1/4 teaspoon salt
- 1 teaspoon baking powder
- 2 tablespoons cocoa powder
- 1/4 teaspoon baking soda
- 1/2 cup dark chocolate chips
- 1/4 cup pistachios, cracked (optional)
- Cooking spray
- Muffin pan or baking cups

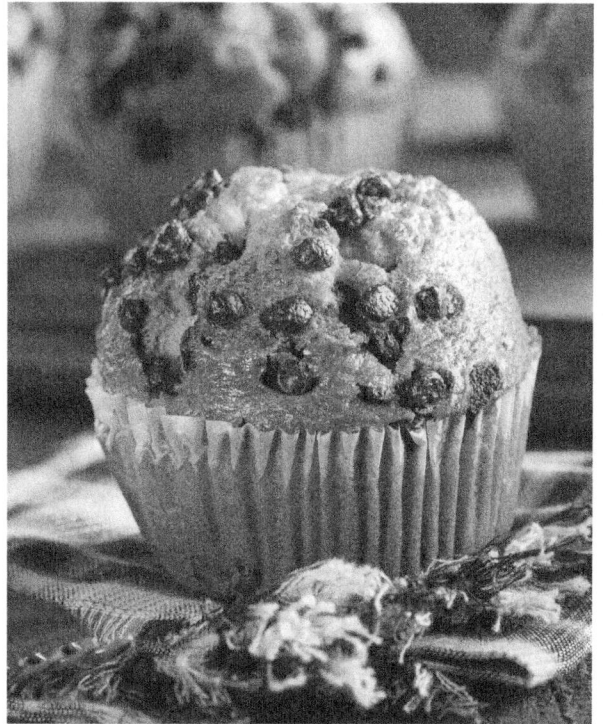

DIRECTIONS

1. In a bowl, mix sugar, coconut/soy milk, coconut oil, and vanilla extractthen set aside.
2. In a second bowl, mix together flour, cocoa powder, baking powder, baking soda, and salt.
3. Mix the dry ingredients into the wet ingredients gradually, until smooth. Then fold in chocolate chips and pistachios.
4. Preheat the Air Fryer for 300°F in 4 mins.
5. Grease muffin cups with cooking spray and pour in batter until cups are 3/4 full.
6. Put the muffins into the preheated air fryer. Bake muffin for 300°F in 15 minutes. Then take out, let cool and serve.

Chocolate Espresso Muffins

🍴 Servings: 8   🕐 25 minutes

INGREDIENTS

- 1 large egg
- 1 cup all-purpose flour
- 3/4 cup light brown sugar
- 3/4 cup milk
- 1/2 cup cocoa powder
- 1/2 teaspoon baking soda
- 1/2 teaspoon baking powder
- 1/2 teaspoon instant espresso powder
- 1/4 teaspoon salt
- 1/2 cup vegetable oil
- 1 teaspoon vanilla extract
- 1 teaspoon apple cider vinegar
- Cooking spray
- Muffin pan or baking cups.

DIRECTIONS

1. In a large bowl, mix the flour, cocoa powder, light brown sugar, baking powder, espresso powder, baking soda, and salt.
2. In second bowl, whisk the egg, milk, vanilla extract, apple cider vinegar, and vegetable oil.
3. Mix the wet ingredients with the dry until combined.
4. Grease the muffin cups with cooking spray and pour in batter until cups are 3/4 full. Put the muffins into the preheated air fryer. Bake muffin for 300°F in 15 minutes.
5. Then take out, let cool and serve.

Orange Cranberry Muffins

🍴 Servings: 6   🕐 25 minutes

INGREDIENTS

- 1 egg.
- 1/4 cup sugar.
- 1 cup all-purpose flour.
- 1/4 teaspoon salt.
- 1 cup cranberries.
- 1 teaspoon baking powder.
- 1/4 teaspoon baking soda.
- 1/4 cup orange juice.
- 1/4 cup vegetable oil.
- 1 orange, zested.
- Cooking spray.
- 1 (6-cup) muffin pan or baking cups

DIRECTIONS

1. In a large bowl, mix well the flour, sugar, baking powder, baking soda, salt, and cranberries .
2. In second bowl, whisk the egg, orange juice, vegetable oil, and orange zest. Then mix the wet ingredients with the dry ingredients until combined.
3. Grease the muffin cups with cooking spray and pour in batter until cups are 3/4 full. Put the muffins carefully into the preheated air fryer. Bake muffin for 300°F in 15 minutes.
4. Take out, let cool and serve.

Banana Nut Muffins

🍴 Servings: 6   🕐 40 minutes

INGREDIENTS

- 200g Egg Whites.
- 400g Banana.
- 12g Baking Powder.
- 100g Unsweetened Vanilla Almond Milk.
- 30g Crushed Walnuts.
- 45g Coconut Flour .
- 90g PEScience Gourmet Vanilla Select Protein.
- 45g PB Party Protein Cookie Butter Powder.
- 12g Zero Cal Sweetener of your Choice.
- 5g Ground Cinnamon.

DIRECTIONS

1. In a large bowl, mash your banana until there aren't any chunks, then mix in your egg whites.
2. Mix your dry ingredients together in another, then combine the dry ingredients with the wet.
3. Spray your muffin tins with nonstick cooking spray and evenly add your batter to each. Add your muffins to the air fryer for 30 minutes at 250 degrees F until the tops start cracking and you see some golden-brown spots.
4. Take the muffins out of your air fryer, let them cool, then enjoy.

Note: *If want to lower the calories and fats a good bit, just take out the walnuts!*

Cheesy Cornbread Muffins

🍴 Servings: 6   🕐 25 minutes

INGREDIENTS

- 1 egg
- 1/2 cup all-purpose flour.
- 1 cup corn
- 1/2 cup cornmeal
- 1/2 cup milk
- 3 tablespoons white sugar
- 1 teaspoon salt
- 1.5 teaspoons baking powder
- 3 tablespoons butter, melted
- 3 scallions, chopped
- 3 ounces cheddar cheese, grated
- Cooking spray
- Muffin pan or baking cups

DIRECTIONS

1. In a bowl, mix flour, cornmeal, sugar, salt, and baking powder.
2. Whisk together milk, butter, and egg until well combined.
3. Combine dry ingredients with wet ingredients. Fold in corn, scallions, and cheddar cheese.
4. Grease muffin cups with cooking spray and pour in batter until cups are 3/4 full. Put the muffins into the preheated air fryer. Bake muffin for 300°F in 15 minutes.
5. Then take out, let cool and serve.

Oats Muffins

🍴 Servings: 6   🕐 18 minutes

DIRECTIONS

1. Mix the dry ingredients together to get a acrumbly mixture.
2. Divide the milk into two equal parts, then add one to the baking soda and the other to the vinegar.
3. Mix both milk mixtures together and wait until the milk starts to foam. Add this mixture to the crumb mixture and start whisking the ingredients at a high speed.
4. Once you have a smooth batter, pour the mixture into the muffin cups. Preheat the fryer to 300 degrees F for 5 minutes. Then place the muffin cups in the basket and bake at 320 degrees F for 15 minutes Remove and serve hot.

INGREDIENTS

- 2 cups All-purpose flour.
- 1.5 cup milk.
- 1/2 tsp baking powder.
- 1/2 tsp baking soda
- 2 tbsp butter.
- 1 cup sugar.
- 3 tsp vinegar.
- 1 cup oats.
- 1/2 tsp vanilla essence.
- Muffin cups or butter paper cups.

Pumpkin Muffins

🍴 Servings: 18   🕐 25 minutes

INGREDIENTS

- 1/4 cup butter.
- 1/2 teaspoon baking powder.
- 1/4 cup flour.
- 1/2 cup sugar.
- 3/4 cup pumpkin puree.
- 1 teaspoon cinnamon powder.
- 2 tablespoons flaxseed meal.
- 1/2 teaspoon nutmeg, ground.
- 1 egg.
- 1/2 teaspoon baking soda.

DIRECTIONS

1. Mix butter with pumpkin puree and egg in a bowl, and blend well.
2. Add flaxseed meal, sugar, flour, baking powder, baking soda, nutmeg and cinnamon and stir well.
3. Use a spoon to scoop the mixture into the muffin cups. Then put them in your air fryer at 350 degrees F and bake for 15 minutes.
4. Serve muffins cold as a snack.

Simple Donut

INGREDIENTS

- 4 tablespoons butter, soft.
- 1/2 cup sour cream.
- 1.5 teaspoon baking powder.
- 2 egg yolks.
- 2.25 cups white flour.
- 1 teaspoon cinnamon powder.
- 1/2 cup sugar.
- 1/3 cup caster sugar.

DIRECTIONS

1. Mix 2 tablespoons of butter with simple sugar and egg yolks and beat well in a bowl.
2. Add half of the sour cream to the bowl and stir.
3. In another bowls, mix flour with baking powder, stir. Then add the egg mixture in step 1 and 2 and stir well
4. Stir until you obtain a dough, transfer it to a floured working surface, roll it out and cut big circles with smaller ones in the middle.
5. Brush doughnuts with the rest of the butter, heat up your air fryer at 360 degrees F in 3 minutes, place doughnuts inside and bake them for 8 minutes.
6. Mix cinnamon with caster sugar in a bowl.
7. Arrange doughnuts on plates and dip them in cinnamon sugar mixture before serving.

Vanilla Mini Donuts

Servings: 27   25 minutes

INGREDIENTS

- 412g Egg Whites
- 75g All Purpose Flour
- 75g Whey/Casein Blend Vanilla Protein Powder
- 15g Baking Powder
- 36g Birthday Cake Batter Protein Cookie Butter Powder
- 30g Coconut Flour
- 15g Zero Cal Sweetener of your choice
- 412g Plain Nonfat Greek Yogurt
- 150g Unsweetened Apple Sauce

DIRECTIONS

1. Add all your dry ingredients into a bowl and mix well to avoid clumping. Then add your wet ingredients and mix until combined.
2. Add mini donut silicone molds to your air fryer and spray with non stick cooking spray.
3. Add your batter to each leaving a little bit from the top because these will rise. Bake for 250 degrees F in 15 minutes, then open the air fryer, flip the other side of the bagel, bake for 5 more minutes at the same temperature.
4. Then add whatever frosting your heart desires on top along with toppings and enjoy!

Everything Bagels

🍴 Servings: 6   🕐 15 minutes

INGREDIENTS

- 50g Egg Whites
- 45g All Purpose Flour
- 3g Baking Powder
- 8g Coconut Flour
- 3g Everything Bagel Seasoning
- 100g Plain Nonfat Greek Yogurt

DIRECTIONS

1. In a bowl, mix all of your dry ingredients together, then add in your wet ingredients and mix everything together.
2. Spray mini silicone bagel molds with nonstick cooking spray and evenly spread your batter to each.
3. Air fry the bagels at 360 degrees F for 8 minutes, then open the air fryer, flip the other side of the bagel, bake for another 4-6 minutes until golden.
4. When they're done, let the bagels cool on a cooling rack. Don't cut them out right away as they will be super soft in the middle.

Strawberry Donuts

Servings: 4   25 minutes

INGREDIENTS

- 8 ounces flour.
- 1 tablespoon brown sugar.
- 1 tablespoon white sugar.
- 1 egg.
- 2.5 tablespoons butter.
- 4 ounces whole milk.
- 1 teaspoon baking powder.

For the strawberry icing:
- 2 tablespoons butter.
- 3.5 ounces icing sugar.
- ½ teaspoon pink coloring.
- ¼ cup strawberries, chopped.
- 1 tablespoon whipped cream.

DIRECTIONS

1. Mix butter, 1 tablespoon brown sugar, 1 tablespoon white sugar and flour in a bowl and stir.
2. In another bowl, mix egg with 1.5 tablespoons butter and milk and stir well.
3. Combine the 2 mixtures, stir, shape donuts from this mix, place them in your air fryer's basket and bake at 360 degrees F for 15-18 minutes.
4. Put 1 tablespoon butter, icing sugar, food coloring, whipped cream and strawberry puree and whisk well.
5. Arrange donuts on a platter and pour the strawberry sauce on top and enjoy.

Coconut Donuts

🍴 Servings: 4   🕐 25 minutes

INGREDIENTS

- 1 large egg.
- 1.5 cups all-purpose flour.
- 1/2 cup buttermilk.
- 3 tbsp (45g) unsalted butter, melted.
- 1/2 cup unsweetened shredded coconut.
- 1/2 cup sweetened shredded coconut, for coating.
- 1/2 cup granulated sugar.
- 1 tsp baking powder.
- 1/2 tsp baking soda.
- 1/2 tsp salt.
- 1 tsp vanilla extract.

DIRECTIONS

1. Whisk together flour, unsweetened shredded coconut, sugar, baking powder, baking soda, and salt in a bowl.
2. In another bowl, whisk together the buttermilk, eggs, vanilla extract, and melted butter. Blend dry ingredients into wet ingredients and stir until combined.
3. Scoop the batter into the greased donut pan, filling each pan about 2/3 full. Place them in the air fryer and bake at 360°F for 12-15 minutes.
4. Remove the donuts from the basket and let cool, rolling each donut in a dish of grated coconut to coat. Enjoy !

Coffee Donuts

🍴 Servings: 4   🕐 25 minutes

INGREDIENTS

- 1 large egg.
- 1.5 cups all-purpose flour.
- 1/2 cup buttermilk.
- 3 tbsp (45g) unsalted butter, melted.
- 1/2 cup unsweetened shredded coconut.
- 1/2 cup sweetened shredded coconut, for coating.
- 1/2 cup granulated sugar.
- 1 tsp baking powder.
- 1/2 tsp baking soda.
- 1/2 tsp salt.
- 1 tsp vanilla extract.

DIRECTIONS

1. Mix flour, sugar, baking powder, baking soda and salt in a bowl.
2. In the second bowl, mix the cooled coffee, eggs, vanilla extract, and melted butter. Blend dry ingredients into wet ingredients and stir until combined.
3. Pour the dough into the donut mold. Place the filled mold in the air fryer and bake at 380°F for 10-12 minutes.
4. Remove the donuts from the air fryer and let cool for a few minutes before removing from the pan. Roll each donut in a plate of coffee or cocoa powder for coating. Enjoy !

Lemon Poppyseed Donuts

🍴 Servings: 4   🕐 25 minutes

INGREDIENTS

- 1 large egg.
- 1.5 cups all-purpose flour.
- 1/2 cup granulated sugar.
- 1/2 cup powdered sugar, for coating.
- 1/2 cup buttermilk.
- 1 tsp baking powder.
- 1/2 tsp baking soda.
- 1/2 tsp salt.
- 3 tbsp unsalted butter, melted.
- 2 tbsp lemon zest.
- 2 tbsp poppy seeds.
- 1 tsp vanilla extract.

DIRECTIONS

1. Mix flour, sugar, baking powder, baking soda and salt in a bowl.
2. In another bowl, whisk together the buttermilk, eggs, vanilla extract, melted butter, lemon zest, and poppy seeds. Mix dry ingredients into wet ingredients and stir until just combined.
3. Pour the dough into the donut mold. Place the filled mold in the air fryer and cook at 380°F for 10-12 minutes.
4. Remove the donuts from the air fryer and let cool for a few minutes before removing from the pan. Roll each donut in the sugar dish to coat. Enjoy !

Carrot Donuts

🍴 Servings: 4   🕐 25 minutes

INGREDIENTS

- 1 large egg.
- 1.5 cups all-purpose flour.
- 1/2 cup granulated sugar.
- 1 tsp baking powder.
- 1/2 tsp baking soda.
- 1/2 tsp salt.
- 1/2 cup buttermilk.
- 3 tbsp unsalted butter, melted.
- 1 cup grated carrots.
- 1/2 cup chopped pecans, for coating.
- 1 tsp cinnamon.
- 1 tsp vanilla extract.

DIRECTIONS

1. Mix flour, sugar, baking powder, baking soda and salt in a bowl.
2. In another bowl, whisk together the buttermilk, eggs, vanilla extract, melted butter, grated carrots, and cinnamon. Mix dry ingredients with wet ingredients and stir until combined.
3. Pour greased doughnut mold dough. Place the filled mold in the preheated air fryer and bake at 380°F for 10-12 minutes.
4. Remove the donuts from the air fryer and let cool for a few minutes before removing from the pan.
5. Place the chopped pecans on a plate. Roll each donut in pecans to coat. Enjoy!

Simple Cookies

🍴 Servings: 12 🕐 20 minutes

INGREDIENTS

- 1 large egg.
- 1 cup (125g) all-purpose flour.
- 1 tsp vanilla extract.
- 3/4 cup (150g) granulated sugar.
- 1/2 tsp baking powder.
- 1/4 tsp salt.
- 1/2 cup (113g) unsalted butter, room temperature.

DIRECTIONS

1. Mix flour, baking powder and salt in a bowl, set aside.
2. In another bowl, beat the buttercream and sugar until light and fluffy then add the eggs and vanilla extract, beating well. Gradually add the dry ingredients in step 1 to the mix until just combined.
3. Use a spoon or spatula to scoop each spoonful of batter onto a parchment lined plate. Place the dough balls in a single layer in the basket of the preheated air fryer.
4. Bake at 330°F (165°C) for 8-10 minutes or until edges are golden brown
5. Remove the cookies from the air fryer and serve to cool.

Brown Butter Cookies

🍴 Servings: 12 🕐 20 minutes

INGREDIENTS

- 2 eggs, whisked.
- 1.5 cups butter.
- 2 cups brown sugar.
- 2/3 cup pecans, chopped.
- 3 cups flour.
- 1 teaspoon baking soda.
- 2 teaspoons vanilla extract.
- 1/2 teaspoon baking powder.

DIRECTIONS

1. Heat up a pan, add butter and cook over medium heat, stir until it melts, add brown sugar and stir until this dissolves.
2. Mix flour with pecans, vanilla extract, baking powder, baking soda, and eggs in a bowl, and stir well.
3. Add brown butter, stir well and arrange spoonfuls of this mix on a lined baking sheet that fits your air fryer.
4. Introduce in the fryer and cook at 340 degrees F for 10 minutes.
5. Leave cookies to cool down and serve.

Potato Chip Cookies

🍴 Servings: 12   🕐 20 minutes

INGREDIENTS

- 1 large egg.
- 1.5 cups all-purpose flour.
- 1 tsp baking powder.
- 1/2 tsp baking soda.
- 1/2 tsp salt.
- 1/2 cup unsalted butter, room temperature.
- 1 cup semisweet chocolate chips.
- 1/2 cup granulated sugar.
- 1/2 cup brown sugar.
- 2 cups crushed potato chips.
- 1 tsp vanilla extract.

DIRECTIONS

1. Whisk together flour, baking powder, baking soda and salt in a bowl.
2. In another bowl, beat the buttercream, granulated sugar, and brown sugar until light and fluffy, add the eggs and vanilla extract, and stir.
3. Gradually add in dry ingredients and mix until just combined. Stir in the fries and chocolate chips.
4. Use a spoon to scoop each scoop of dough onto the prepared baking tray, placing them at least 2 inches apart. Place in a preheated air fryer. Bake cookies at 380°F for 12-15 minutes or until edges are golden brown.
5. Remove cookies from oven and let cool before serving.

Macaroons

🍴 Servings: 20　🕐 18 minutes

INGREDIENTS

- 4 egg whites.
- 2 tablespoons sugar.
- 2 cup coconut, shredded.
- 1 teaspoon vanilla extract.

DIRECTIONS

1. Mix egg whites with stevia and beat using your mixer then pour them into the bowl.
2. Add coconut and vanilla extract, whisk again, shape small balls out of this mix, introduce them in your air fryer and cook at 340 degrees F for 8-10 minutes.
3. Let the macaroons cool completely and serve.

Honey & Oats Cookie

🍴 Servings: 18 🕐 25 minutes

INGREDIENTS

- 1 cups flour
- 1 cup all-purpose flour
- 1/2 cup milk
- 1 tsp baking powder
- 1 tbsp liquid glucose
- 2 tbsp powdered sugar
- 1/2 cup oats
- 1 tbsp unsalted butter
- 2 tsp honey

DIRECTIONS

1. In a bowl, mix the dry ingredients together and warm the glucose with a little water. Mix the glucose, honey and the butter to the bowl followed by the milk.

2. Roll the dough using a pin. Create cookies and set them on a prepared baking tray.

3. Preheat the fryer to 300 Fahrenheit for 4 minutes. Then put the baking tray in the basket and bake to 250 Fahrenheit in 15 minutes. Turn the cookies in the tray to ensure that they are cooked uniformly.

4. When the cookies have cooled, store them in an airtight container and serve

Custards Cookie

INGREDIENTS

- 2 tbsp margarine.
- 1 cup all-purpose flour
- 1/2 cup custard powder
- 1/2 cup icing sugar
- A pinch of baking soda and baking powder

DIRECTIONS

1. Mix cream the margarine and sugar together. Then add the remaining ingredients and fold them together.
2. Prepare a baking tray greased with butter. Roll the dough into balls, roll the balls in the flour and place in the baking tray. Preheat the fryer to 320 Fahrenheit for 4 minutes.
3. Put the baking tray in the air fryer and bake at 320 degrees F for 10 minutes or when you see the balls have turned golden brown.
4. Remove the tray and let it cool outside for half an hour and serve.

Lentils Cookies

Servings: 36 25 minutes

INGREDIENTS

- 1 egg.
- 1 cup water.
- 1 cup white flour.
- 1 cup canned lentils, drained and mashed.
- 1 teaspoon baking powder.
- 1 teaspoon cinnamon powder.
- 1 cup whole wheat flour.
- 1/2 teaspoon nutmeg, ground.
- 1 cup butter, soft.
- 1/2 cup white sugar.
- 1/2 cup brown sugar.
- 2 teaspoons almond extract.
- 1 cup raisins.
- 1 cup rolled oats.
- 1 cup coconut, unsweetened and shredde.

DIRECTIONS

1. Mix white and whole wheat flour with salt, cinnamon, baking powder and nutmeg in a bowl and stir.
2. In second bowl, mix butter with white and brown sugar and stir using your kitchen mixer for 2 minutes.
3. Add egg, almond extract, lentils mix, flour mix, oats, raisins and coconut and stir everything well.
4. Scoop tablespoons of dough on a lined baking sheet that fits your air fryer, introduce them in the fryer and cook at 350 degrees F for 18 minutes.
5. Arrange cookies on a serving platter and serve.

Pumpkin Cookies

🍴 Servings: 24 🕐 25 minutes

INGREDIENTS

- 1/4 cup honey.
- 2.5 cups flour.
- 2 tablespoons butter.
- 1/2 teaspoon baking soda.
- 1 tablespoon flax seed, ground.
- 3 tablespoons water.
- 1/2 cup pumpkin flesh, mashed.
- 1/2 cup dark chocolate chips.
- 1 teaspoon vanilla extract.

DIRECTIONS

1. Mix flax seed with water in a bowl, stir and leave aside for a few minutes.
2. In second bowl, mix flour with salt and baking soda.
3. In a third bowl, mix honey with pumpkin puree, butter, vanilla extract and flaxseed.
4. Combine flour with honey mix and chocolate chips and stir.
5. Scoop 1 tablespoon of cookie dough on a lined baking sheet that fits your air fryer, repeat with the rest of the dough, introduce them in your air fryer and cook at 330 degrees F for 18 minutes.
6. Leave cookies to cool down and serve.

Thin and Crispy
Chocolate Chip Cookies

🍴 Servings: 20 🕐 30 minutes

INGREDIENTS

- 2 large eggs.
- 2 cups chocolate chips.
- 2.25 cups all-purpose flour.
- 1 tsp baking soda.
- 1 tsp salt.
- 1 cup unsalted butter, room temperature.
- 3/4 cup granulated sugar.
- 3/4 cup brown sugar.
- 2 tsp vanilla extract.

DIRECTIONS

1. Mix flour, baking soda and salt in a bowl.
2. In the second bowl, whisk together the buttercream, granulated sugar, and brown sugar until smooth and fluffy. Crack the eggs one at a time, then add the vanilla extract and beat well. Gradually add in dry ingredients and mix until just combined. Add the chocolate chips and stir well.
3. Cover the dough and refrigerate for at least 2 hours or overnight.
4. Use a spoon to scoop each scoop of dough onto the prepared baking tray, placing them at least 2 inches apart (For thin and crispy cookie, be sure to flatten the dough balls). Then place in the preheated air fryer basket. Bake at 380°F for 8-10 minutes or until edges are golden brown
5. Take the cookies out of the oven and let it cool completely before serving.

Malted Chocolate Chip Cookie Bars

🍴 Servings: 20   🕐 30 minutes

INGREDIENTS

- 2 large eggs.
- 2.25 cups all-purpose flour.
- 2 cups chocolate chips.
- 1 tsp baking powder.
- 1/2 tsp baking soda.
- 1/2 tsp salt.
- 1 cup (226g) unsalted butter, room temperature.
- 3/4 cup (150g) granulated sugar.
- 3/4 cup (150g) brown sugar.
- 1/2 cup malted milk powder.
- 2 tsp vanilla extract.

DIRECTIONS

1. Mix flour, baking powder, baking soda and salt in a bowl.
2. In another bowl, beat the buttercream, granulated sugar, and brown sugar until smooth and creamy, then stir in the eggs, vanilla extract, and malted milk powder. Gradually add in dry ingredients and mix until just combined. Add the chocolate chips and stir well.
3. Spread batter evenly onto greased baking dish, place in preheated air fryer, bake at 350°F for 25-30 minutes or until edges are golden brown.
4. Remove the bars from the air fryer and let them cool, cut the bars into squares and serve.

Lemon Poppy Seed Tea Cookies

🍴 Servings: 20 🕐 30 minutes

INGREDIENTS

- 1 large egg.
- 2 tbsp poppy seeds.
- 2.25 cups all-purpose flour.
- 1 tsp baking powder.
- 1/4 tsp baking soda.
- 1/2 tsp salt.
- 1 cup unsalted butter, room temperature.
- 3/4 cup granulated sugar.
- 1 tsp vanilla extract.
- 1 tbsp grated lemon zest.
- 2 tbsp freshly squeezed lemon juice.

DIRECTIONS

1. Mix flour, baking powder, baking soda and salt in a bowl.
2. In another bowl, beat cream butter and sugar until smooth and fluffy. Crack in the eggs, then stir in the vanilla extract, lemon juice and lemon zest. Gradually add in dry ingredients and mix until just combined. Stir in the poppy seeds.
3. Use a spoon to scoop each scoop of dough onto the prepared baking tray, placing them at least 2 inches apart. Place the tray in the preheated air fryer basket. Bake cookies at 350°F for 8-10 minutes or until edges are golden brown
4. Remove cookies from air fryer and let cool before serving.

Orange Cookies

🍴 Servings: 8 🕐 20 minutes

INGREDIENTS

- 1 egg, whisked.
- 2 cups flour.
- 3/4 cup sugar.
- 1 teaspoon baking powder.
- 1/2 cup butter, soft.
- 1 tablespoon orange zest, grated.
- 1 teaspoon vanilla extract.

For the filling:
- 4 ounces cream cheese, soft.
- 2 cups powdered sugar.
- 1/2 cup butter.

DIRECTIONS

1. Mix cream cheese with 1/2 cup butter and 2 cups powdered sugar in a bowl, stir well using your mixer and leave aside for now.
2. In second bowl, mix flour with baking powder.
3. In another bowl, mix 1/2 cup butter with 3/4 cup sugar, egg, vanilla extract and orange zest and whisk well.
4. Combine flour with orange mix, stir well and scoop 1 tablespoon of the mix on a lined baking sheet that fits your air fryer.
5. Repeat with the rest of the orange batter, introduce in the fryer and cook at 340 degrees F for 12 minutes.
6. Leave cookies to cool down, spread cream filling on half of them top with the other cookies and serve.

Chocolate Chip Cookies

INGREDIENTS

- 1/2 cup unsalted butter, softened
- 1/3 cup granulated sugar
- 1/3 cup light brown sugar
- 1 large egg
- 1/2 tsp. vanilla extract
- 1 cup plus 1 tbsp. flour
- 1/2 tsp. baking powder
- 1/4 tsp. baking soda
- 1/2 tsp salt
- 1/4 cup semisweet chocolate chips
- 1/4 cup milk chocolate chips
- 1/4 cup white chocolate chips
- 1/2 cup chopped & toasted walnut pieces

DIRECTIONS

1. Whip together the butter, granulated sugar, and brown sugar using an electric mixer. Add the egg and vanilla and mix well.
2. In another bowl, combine the flour, baking powder, baking soda, and salt. Slowly mix the dry mixture into the butter mixture until creamy.
3. Add all the chocolate chips and walnut pieces to the mixture and mix. Refrigerate the dough for 1 hr.
4. Shape the dough into 1-in balls, Put the balls in an air fryer lined with baking paper and flatten each ball slightly.
5. Baking at 325 degrees F for 18 minutes. Flip the other side of the cookies while baking (9 mins).
6. Let the cookies cool before serving.

Peanut Butter Cookies

🍴 Servings: 12 🕐 30 minutes

INGREDIENTS

- 1 large egg.
- 250g creamy peanut butter.
- 1.5 cups all-purpose flour.
- 1 tsp baking powder.
- 1/2 tsp baking soda.
- 1/2 tsp salt.
- 100g granulated sugar.
- 100g brown sugar.
- 1 tsp vanilla extract.

DIRECTIONS

1. Mix flour, baking powder, baking soda and salt in a bowl.
2. In a large bowl, mix peanut butter, granulated sugar, and brown sugar together until well combined. Add eggs, vanilla extract and stir well. Gradually add in dry ingredients and mix until just combined.
3. Use a spoon to scoop each cookie dough onto a greased baking tray, flattening each cookie with a fork to form a cross. Then place the tray in the air fryer basket, making sure to leave some space between the cookies.
4. Bake cookies at 330°F for 8-10 minutes or until edges are lightly golden brown.
5. Remove cookies from air fryer and let cool before serving.

Trail Mix Cookies

🍴 Servings: 12 🕐 30 minutes

DIRECTIONS

- 2 large eggs.
- 2.25 cups all-purpose flour.
- 1 tsp baking powder.
- 1/2 tsp baking soda.
- 1/2 tsp salt.
- 1 cup unsalted butter, room temperature.
- 2 cups semisweet chocolate chips.
- 150g chopped nuts (such as almonds, pecans, or walnuts)
- 120g dried fruit (such as raisins, cranberries, or chopped dates)

- 150g rolled oats.
- 150g granulated sugar.
- 150g brown sugar.
- 1 tsp vanilla extract.

INGREDIENTS

1. Mix flour, baking powder, baking soda and salt in a bowl.
2. In another bowl, beat the buttercream, brown sugar, and granulated sugar until light and fluffy. Add eggs, vanilla extract and mix well. Gradually add in dry ingredients and mix until just combined. Add chocolate chips, nuts, dried fruit, and oats to the mixture until evenly distributed.
3. Scoop each scoop of dough onto the prepared baking tray, placing them at least 2 inches apart. Then put in the preheated air fryer.
4. Bake at 380°F for 12-15 minutes or until edges are lightly golden brown.
5. Remove cookies from oven and let cool before serving.

Buttermilk Biscuits

YI Servings: 4   🕐 25 minutes

INGREDIENTS

- 1.25 cup white flour.
- 1 teaspoon sugar.
- ½ cup self-rising flour.
- ¼ teaspoon baking soda.
- ¾ cup buttermilk Maple syrup for serving.
- ½ teaspoon baking powder.
- 4 tablespoons butter, cold and cubed+ 1 tablespoon melted butter.

DIRECTIONS

1. Mix white flour with self-rising flour, baking soda, baking powder and sugar and stir in a bowl.
2. Add cold butter to the bowl and stir well with the above mixture.
3. Add buttermilk, stir until you obtain a dough and transfer to a floured surface.
4. Roll your dough and cut 10 pieces using a round cutter.
5. Arrange biscuits in your air fryer's cake pan, brush them with melted butter and cook at 400 degrees F for 8 minutes.
6. Serve them for breakfast with some maple syrup on top.

Casserole Biscuits
with Sausage

Servings: 8   25 minutes

INGREDIENTS

- 12 ounces biscuits, quartered.
- A pinch of salt and black pepper.
- 3 tablespoons flour
- 2.5 cups milk
- ½ pound sausage, chopped.
- Cooking spray.

DIRECTIONS

1. Mix softened butter with sugar, vanilla and cinnamon and beat well in a bowl.
2. Spread this on bread slices, place them in your air fryer and cook at 400 degrees F for 4-5 minutes.
3. Divide among plates and serve.

Cheddar Biscuits

Y¶ Servings: 8　🕐 20 minutes

INGREDIENTS

- 2.3 cup self-rising flour.
- 1 cup flour.
- 1/2 cup + 1 tablespoon butter, melted.
- 1/2 cup cheddar cheese, grated.
- 2 tablespoons sugar.
- 1.3 cup buttermilk.

DIRECTIONS

1. Mix self-rising flour with 1/2 cup butter, sugar, cheddar cheese and buttermilk in a bowl, and stir until you obtain a dough.
2. Spread 1 cup flour out a surface, roll dough, flatten it, cut 8 circles with a cookie cutter and coat them with flour.
3. Line air fryer's basket with tin foil, add biscuits, brush them with melted butter and cook them at 380 degrees F for 20 minutes.
4. Enjoy!

Plum and Currant Tart

🍴 Servings: 6   🕐 45 minutes

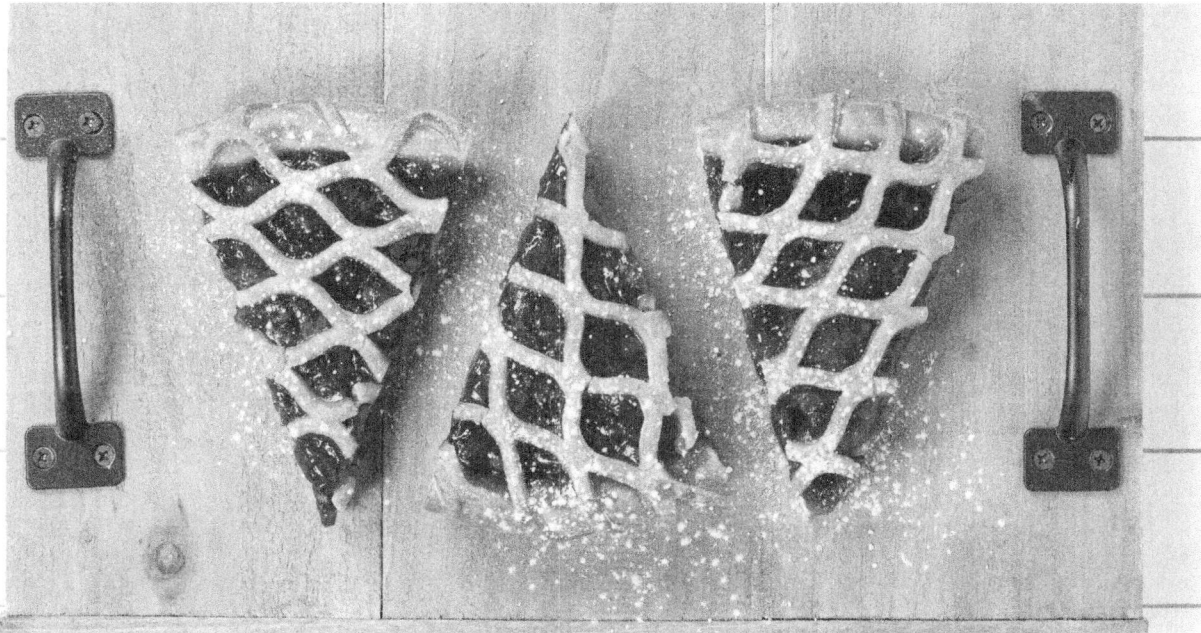

INGREDIENTS

For the crumble:
- 3 tablespoons milk.
- 1 cup brown rice flour
- 1/4 cup almond flour.
- 1/4 cup millet flour.
- 1/2 cup cane sugar.
- 10 tablespoons butter, soft.

For the filling:
- 1 cup white currants.
- 1 pound small plums, pitted and halved.
- 1/4 teaspoon ginger powder.
- 2 tablespoons cornstarch.
- 1 teaspoon lime juice.
- 3 tablespoons sugar.
- 1/2 teaspoon vanilla extract.
- 1/2 teaspoon cinnamon powder.

DIRECTIONS

1. Mix brown rice flour with 1/2 cup sugar, millet flour, almond flour, butter and milk in a bowl and stir until you obtain a sand like dough.
2. Reserve 1/4 of the dough, press the rest of the dough into a tart pan that fits your air fryer and keep in the fridge for 30 minutes.
3. Meanwhile, in a bowl, mix plums with currants, 3 tablespoons sugar, cornstarch, vanilla extract, cinnamon, ginger and lime juice and stir well.
4. Pour this over tart crust, crumble reserved dough on top, introduce in your air fryer and cook at 350 degrees F for 35 minutes.
5. Leave tart to cool down and serve.

Blueberry Tarts

Servings: 10 · 25 minutes

INGREDIENTS

- 2 tbsp powdered sugar
- 1.5 cup plain flour
- 3 tbsp unsalted butter
- 1 tbsp sliced cashew
- 2 cups cold water

For filling:
- 3 tbsp butter
- 1 cup fresh cream
- 1 cup fresh blueberries (Sliced)

DIRECTIONS

1. Mix well the ingredients together to form a crumbly mixture. Knead the mixture with cold milk and wrap it.
2. Roll the dough into two large circles and place the dough in the cake pan and poke the edges of the dough with a fork.
3. Heat the filling ingredients over low heat and pour over the dough in the tin. Then cover pie tin with the second round.
4. Preheat the fryer to 300 Fahrenheit for 4 minutes. Put the tin in the basket and cover it. bake at 300 Fahrenheit in 8 minutes. When the pastry has turned golden brown, you will need to remove the tin and let it cool. Cut into slices and serve with a dollop of cream.

Chocolate Tarts

🍴 Servings: 8   🕐 25 minutes

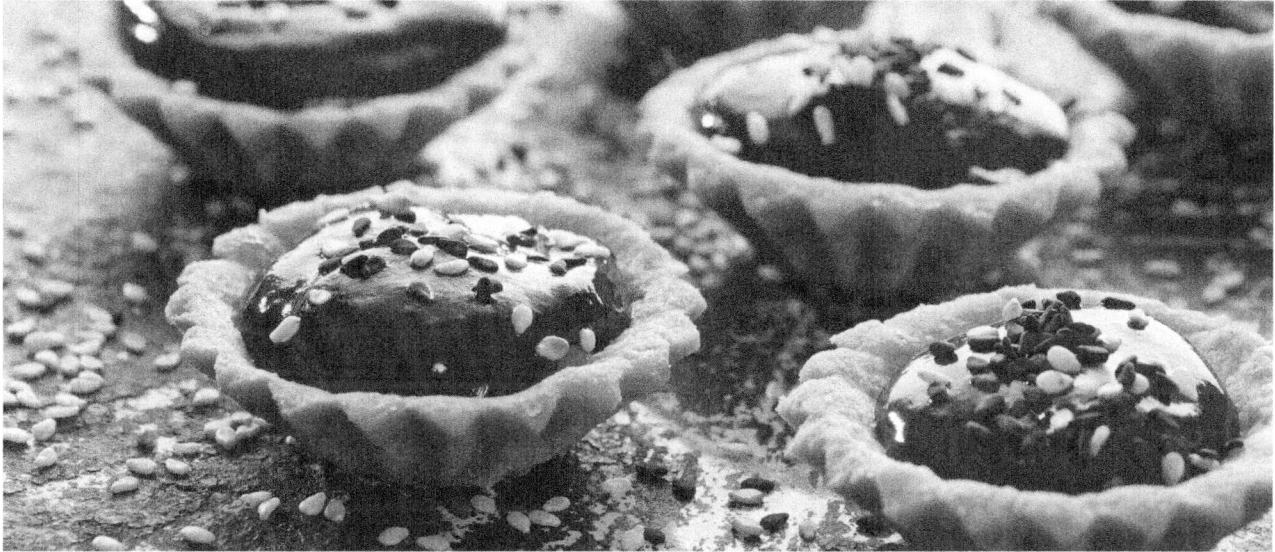

INGREDIENTS

- 1.5 cup plain flour
- 2 cups cold water
- 1/2 cup cocoa powder.
- 2 tbsp powdered sugar
- 3 tbsp unsalted butter
- 1 tbsp sliced cashew

For Truffle filling:
- 3 tbsp butter
- 1.5 melted chocolate
- 1 cup fresh cream

DIRECTIONS

1. Mix the flour, butter, cocoa powder and sugar in a large bowl, . The mixture should resemble breadcrumbs. Knead the dough using the cold milk and wrap it and leave it to cool for 10 minutes.
2. Roll the dough out into the pie and prick the sides of the pie.
3. Mix the ingredients for the filling in another bowl. Make sure that it is a little thick. Add the filling to the pie and cover it with the second round. Put pie into the tin,
4. Preheat the fryer to 300 Fahrenheit for 4 minutes. Put the tin in the basket and cover it. bake at 300 Fahrenheit in 8 minutes. When the pastry has turned golden brown, you will need to remove the tin and let it cool. Cut into slices and serve with a dollop of cream.

Strawberry Jam Tarts

🍴 Servings: 9   🕐 18 minutes

INGREDIENTS

- Strawberry Jam Water
- 100g Butter
- 225g Plain Flour
- 25g Caster Sugar

DIRECTIONS

1. Mix sugar, flour, and butter in a large bowl. Then rub the fat into the sugar and flour until the mixture resembles breadcrumbs.
2. Add water until you have a soft dough.
3. Grease the bottom and sides of the mini cake pan, pour the batter into the cake pan, top with 2 teaspoons of strawberry (or raspberry) jam, and place in the preheated air fryer. Cook for 10 minutes at 180 degrees Celsius or until the cake is cooked through.
4. Take out the cake to cool and serve.

Lemon Tart

🍴 Servings: 6   🕐 35 minutes

INGREDIENTS

For the crust:
- 2 cups white flour.
- 2 tablespoons sugar.
- 12 tablespoons cold butter.
- 3 tablespoons ice water.
- A pinch of salt.

For the filling:
- 2 eggs, whisked.
- Juice from 2 lemons.
- Zest from 2 lemons, grated.
- 1.25 cup sugar.
- 10 tablespoons melted and chilled butter.

DIRECTIONS

1. Mix 2 cups flour with a pinch of salt and 2 tablespoons sugar in a bowl and whisk.
2. Add 12 tablespoons butter and the water, knead until you obtain a dough, shape a ball, wrap in foil and keep in the fridge for 1 hour.
3. Transfer dough to a floured surface, flatten it, arrange on the bottom of a tart pan, prick with a fork, keep in the fridge for 20 minutes, introduce in your air fryer at 360 degrees F and bake for 15 minutes.
4. In another bowl, mix 1.25 cup sugar with eggs, 10 tablespoons butter, lemon juice and lemon zest and whisk very well.
5. Pour this into pie crust, spread evenly, introduce in the fryer and cook at 360 degrees F for 20 minutes.
6. Cut and serve.

Fruit Tarts

🍴 Servings: 8   🕐 30 minutes

INGREDIENTS

- 3 tbsp unsalted butter
- 1.5 cup plain flour
- 2 cups cold water
- 1/2 cup cocoa powder
- 1 tbsp sliced cashew
- 2 tbsp powdered sugar

For Truffle filling:
- 3 tbsp butter
- 2 cups mixed sliced fruits
- 1 cup fresh cream

DIRECTIONS

1. Mix all the ingredients together using milk into dough that is soft. Roll the dough out and cut into two circles. Press the dough into the pie tins and prick on all sides using a fork.

2. In a bowl, mix the ingredients for the filling. Make sure that it is a little thick. Add the filling to the pie and cover it with the second round.

3. Preheat the fryer to 300 Fahrenheit for 4 minutes. Put the tin in the basket and cover it, bake at 300 Fahrenheit in 8 minutes . When the pastry has turned golden brown, you will need to remove the tin and let it cool. Cut into slices and serve with a dollop of cream.

INGREDIENTS

Chocolate Souffle

🍴 Servings: 2   🕐 25 minutes

- 2 eggs, yolks separated from whites.
- Butter, for greasing Sugar, for coating.
- 2 tablespoons all-purpose flour.
- 3 ounces bittersweet chocolate, chopped.
- 1/4 cup unsalted butter.
- 3 tablespoons sugar.
- 1/2 teaspoon pure vanilla extract.
- Powdered sugar, for dusting.

Items needed : 2 (6-ounce) ramekins

DIRECTIONS

1. Grease the ramekins with butter. Sprinkle sugar into the ramekins, shaking to spread around, then dumping out the excess.
2. Mix the chocolate and butter in a saucepan over medium heat, stirring until the chocolate is completely melted.
3. Whisk the egg yolks and vanilla extract. Then combine it the melted chocolate to prevent scrambling. Stir until there are no lumps and set aside to cool.
4. Beat the egg whites in another large bowl with an electric mixer at medium speed until they hold soft peaks. Then add the sugar to the egg whites, a little at a time, continuing to beat at medium speed. Once the sugar has been added, increase to high speed until the egg whites whites hold stiff peaks
5. Stir about 1/2 of the egg whites into the chocolate mixture to lighten it first. Then, add the chocolate mixture to the remaining whites, folding in gently but thoroughly.
6. Pour batter into the ramekins and place into the preheated air fryer. Bake in 330°F in 13-15 minutes.
7. Remove when done, dust the souffles with powdered sugar, and serve immediately.

Vanilla Souffle

🍴 Servings: 6　🕐 25 minutes

INGREDIENTS

- 4 egg yolks
- 1/4 cup sugar
- 1/4 cup all-purpose flour
- 1/4 cup butter, softened
- 1 cup whole milk
- 2 teaspoons vanilla extract
- 1 vanilla bean
- 5 egg whites
- 1 ounce sugar
- 1 teaspoon cream of tartar

DIRECTIONS

1. Mix flour and butter until smooth. In a sauce pan, heat the milk and dissolve the sugar. Add vanilla beans and bring to a boil.
2. Add the flour and butter mixture to the boiling milk. Use an electric mixer to beat this mixture vigorously so that there are no lumps. Simmer for a few minutes until the mixture thickens. Remove vanilla beans and cool in refrigerator 10 minutes.
3. While the mixture is cooling, take the 6-ounce ramekins or soufflé. Cover with butter and sprinkle with a little sugar.
4. In another mixing bowl, quickly beat the egg yolks and vanilla extract then combine with the milk mixture.
5. Beat egg whites, sugar and cream of tartar separately until egg whites form a medium firmness. Fold the egg whites into the soufflé base and pour into the prepared baking dishes and smooth off the tops.
6. Put 3 muffins in the cooking basket and cook for 14-16 minutes at 330°F. Serve with powdered sugar on top of soufflé and with chocolate sauce on the side.

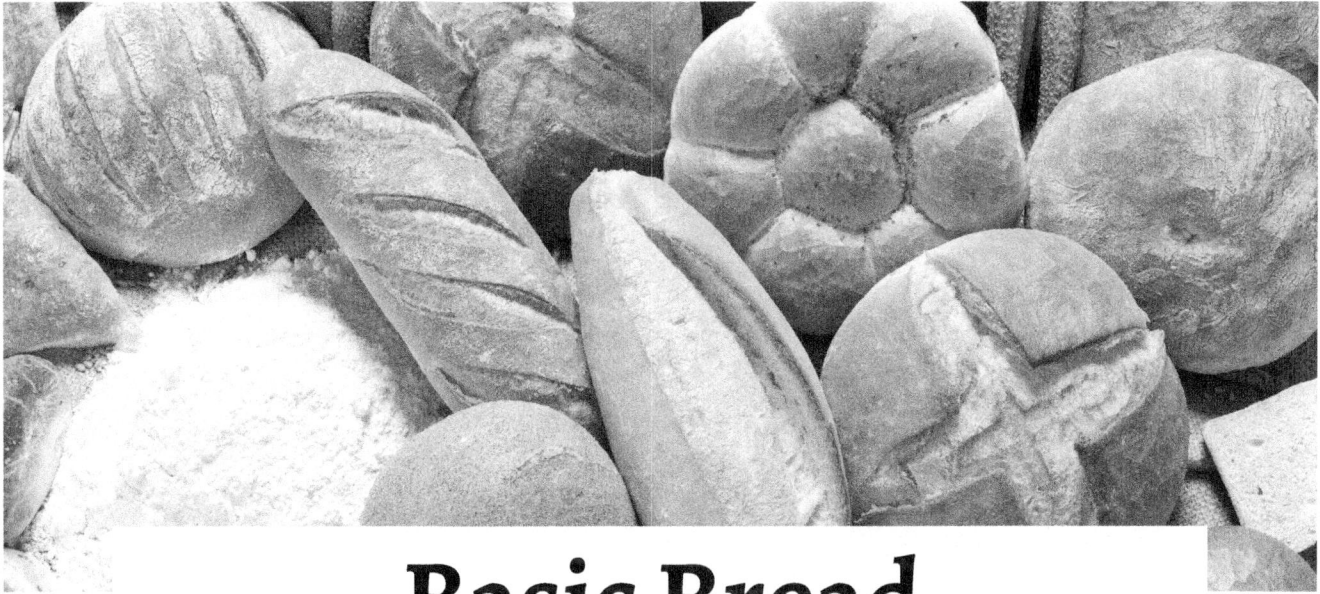

Basic Bread

SERVINGS 2-4	TIME 50 min	DIFFICULTY Easy

INGREDIENTS

- 1 cup all-purpose flour.
- 1/2 cup warm water.
- 1/2 teaspoon sugar.
- 1 teaspoon instant yeast.
- 1 tablespoon olive oil.
- 1/2 teaspoon salt.

DIRECTIONS

1. Mix flour, yeast, salt and sugar in a bowl. Gradually add warm water and olive oil to dry ingredients, stirring until a paste forms.
2. Spread the dough out onto a surface and knead for a few minutes until smooth.
3. Place dough in a greased bowl, cover with cling film and let rise in a warm place for 30 minutes.
4. Roll out the dough on a light dough surface 1/2 inch thick, cut the dough and shape to any shape you like.
5. Place the dough in the preheated air fryer basket, placing the breads not too thick. Bake at 380°F for 8-10 minutes or until golden brown.
6. Serve warm.

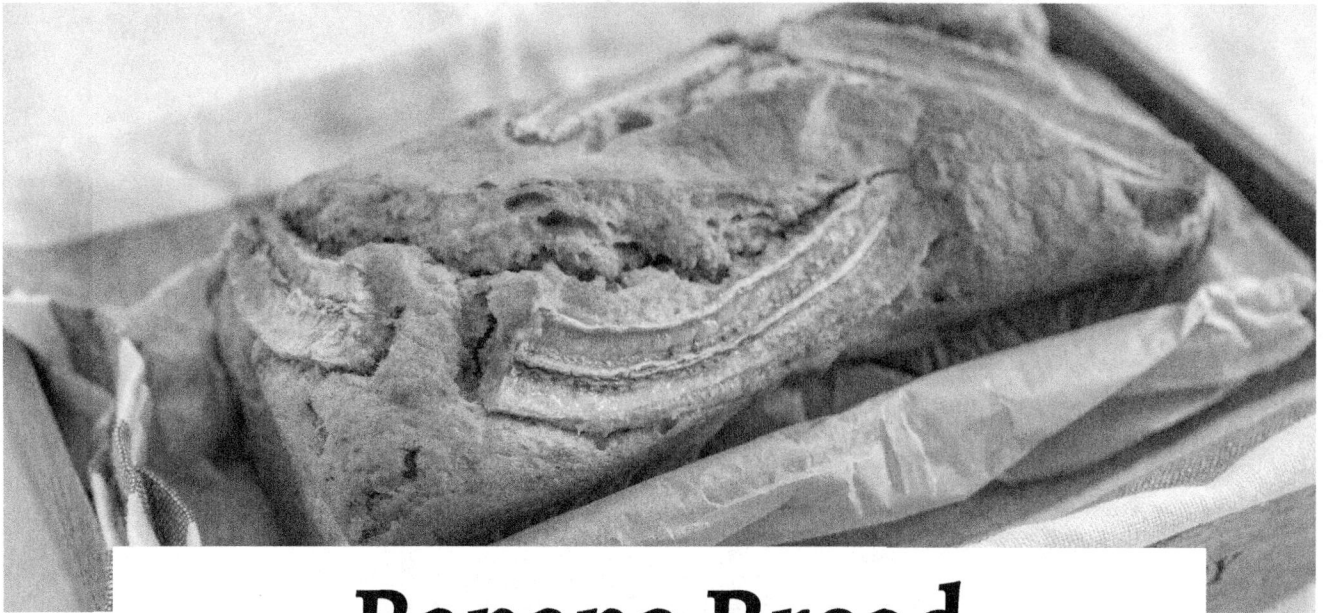

Banana Bread

SERVINGS	TIME	DIFFICULTY
6	50 min	Medium

INGREDIENTS

- 2 bananas, mashed.
- 3/4 cup sugar.
- 1 teaspoon vanilla extract.
- 1/3 cup butter.
- 1.5 cups flour.
- 1 egg.
- 1 teaspoon baking powder.
- 1/2 teaspoons baking soda.
- 1/3 cup milk.
- 1.5 teaspoons cream of tartar.
- Cooking spray.

DIRECTIONS

1. Mix milk with cream of tartar, sugar, butter, egg, vanilla and bananas In a bowl and stir everything.
2. In second bowl, mix flour with baking powder and baking soda.
3. Combine the 2 above mixtures, stir well, pour this into a cake pan greased with some cooking spray.
4. Introduce in your air fryer and cook at 320 degrees F for 38-40 minutes.
5. Take bread out, leave aside to cool down, slice and serve it.

Banana Nut Bread

SERVINGS	TIME	DIFFICULTY
1 Medium Loaf	50 min	Medium

INGREDIENTS

- 1 egg.
- 1/2 cup sugar.
- 1/4 cup unsalted butter, softened.
- 2 overripe bananas, mashed.
- 1/4 teaspoon vanilla extract.
- 1/2 teaspoon baking soda.
- 1/2 cup chopped walnuts.
- 3/4 cups all-purpose flour
- 1/2 teaspoon salt.
- Cooking spray.

Items needed: 1 mini loaf pan

DIRECTIONS

1. Mix Cream together the butter and sugar. Then add egg, mashed bananas, and vanilla extract until well combined. Set aside.
2. Preheat the Air Fryer, adjust temperature to 300°F.
3. Sift together the flour, baking soda, and salt.
4. Fold the dry ingredients into the wet until combined. Mix in the chopped walnuts.
5. Grease the mini loaf pan with cooking spray, then fill with batter. Place into the preheated air fryer.
6. Select the Bake function, adjust time to 40 minutes.
7. Done and serve.

Puff Pastry Cinnamon Swirls

SERVINGS	TIME	DIFFICULTY
9	25 min	Medium

INGREDIENTS

- 1 egg for egg wash
- 1 sheet puff pastry thawed
- 1 cup brown sugar
- 1 teaspoon orange zest
- 1/2 cup salted butter softened
- 1 tablespoon cinnamon
- 1 teaspoon coarse sea salt
- 1 tablespoon coarse sugar to sprinkle on top

Orange Glaze
- 1/4 cup orange juice
- 2 cups powdered sugar
- 2 tablespoons cream
- 1 teaspoon orange zest

Puff Pastry Cinnamon Swirls
(CONTINUE)

DIRECTIONS

1. In a bowl, combine the butter, brown sugar, cinnamon, and orange zestand mix to combine. Spread the cinnamon sugar mixture on top of the puff pastry.
2. Gently roll up the edges and continue rolling, lightly moisten the edges with water or a but of egg wash to make them stick.
3. Using a sharp knife, cut puff pastry in 1 to 1.5" pieces. Then put the pieces on a parchment paper lined baking sheet.
4. Brush the tops of the pastry with the egg wash, then sprinkle with the coarse sugar and sea salt.
5. Bake the cinnamon swirls for 20-25 minutes in 350F degrees or until golden brown. The cinnamon sugar mixture will have leaked into the pan, but that it ok.
6. Remove and spoon the melted cinnamon sugar mixture from the pan over the top of the cinnamon swirls. Let cool for 5 minutes and the bottom will be perfectly caramelized with the cinnamon, sugar and butter mixture.
7. Drizzle with the orange glaze and serve. (Orange Glaze: Combine the orange juice, orange zest, cream and powdered sugar in a bowl and mix to combine)

Pineapple Squash Bread

SERVINGS	TIME	DIFFICULTY
1 Medium Loaf	25 min	Easy

INGREDIENTS

- 275 grams Strong bread flour.
- 1 1/2 tsp Instant dry yeast.
- 2 tbsp Warm water.
- 250 grams Squash puree.
- 1/4 tsp Chili powder.
- 1/2 tsp Salt.
- 1 tbsp Olive oil.
- 1/2 tbsp Curry powder.
- 1 tbsp Cumin.

DIRECTIONS

1. Whisk together warm water and yeast with a mixer. Let stand for 10 minutes to create foam.
2. Mix the squash puree into the flour until it resembles fine breadcrumbs. When yeast is ready, put flour into the bowl and add salt, spices, and oil.
3. Mix and knead until the dough is soft and elastic.
4. Transfer dough into an oiled bowl and let it stand to rise for 1 hour or until doubled in size.
5. Sprinkle flour into loaf tins. Knead the dough again briefly this time with the pineapple chunks and form into a loaf shape. Let stand for 1 hour.
6. Preheat Instant Air Fryer to 190oC.
7. Bake the loaf for 25 minutes.

Nutella Puff Pastry

SERVINGS	TIME	DIFFICULTY
4	25 min	Easy

INGREDIENTS

- 1/2 cup Nutella.
- 1 sheet puff pastry.
- 1 banana, sliced in 1.25" pieces

DIRECTIONS

1. Thaw the puff pastry according to the package instructions.
2. Preheat oven to 380 degrees F.
3. Cut the pastry into 9 squares using a sharp knife. On four squares, place a slice of banana and 2 teaspoons of Nutella on top of the banana.
4. Place the other 4 squares on top and seal the edges. Ensure that the edges are sealed well to avoid leaking while cooking.
5. Bake on a baking sheet for 10-15 minutes, or until light golden brown.
6. Let cool then serve.

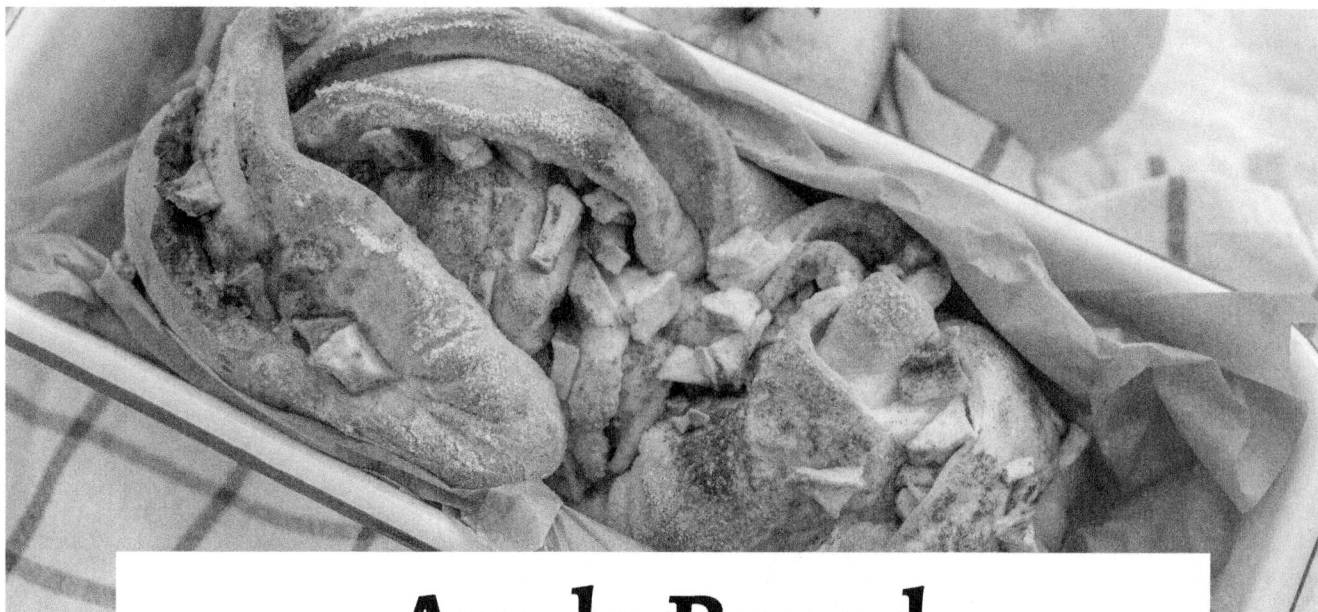

Apple Bread

🍴 SERVINGS 6	🕐 TIME 50 min	👨‍🍳 DIFFICULTY Medium

INGREDIENTS

- 2 eggs.
- 3 cups apples, cored and cubed.
- 1 tablespoon apple pie spice.
- 1 cup sugar.
- 2 cups white flour.
- 1 tablespoon vanilla.
- 1 stick butter.
- 1 tablespoon baking powder.
- 1 cup water.

DIRECTIONS

1. Mix egg with 1 butter stick, apple pie spice and sugar in a bowl and stir using mixer.
2. Add apples to the above mixture and stir again well.
3. In second bowl, mix baking powder with flour and stir.
4. Combine the 2 mixtures, stir and pour into a spring form pan.
5. Put spring form pan in your air fryer and cook at 320 degrees F for 40 minutes.
6. Slice and serve.

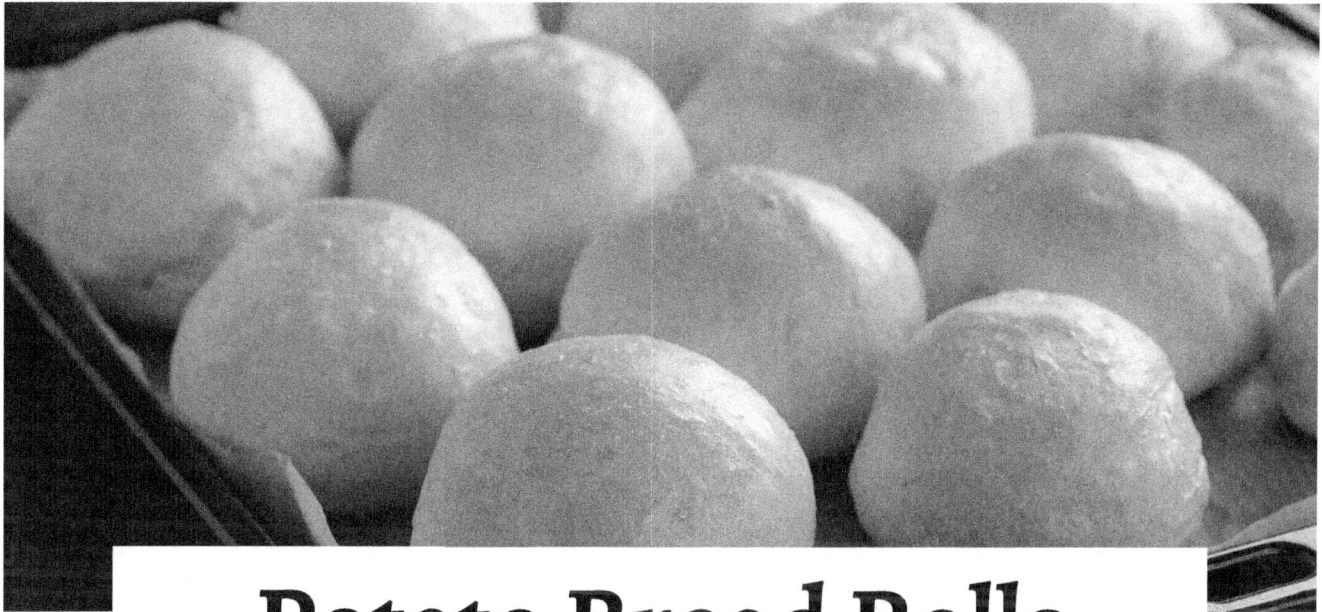

Potato Bread Rolls

SERVINGS	TIME	DIFFICULTY
4	20 min	Medium

INGREDIENTS

- 5 potatoes, boiled, peeled and mashed.
- 2 tablespoons olive oil Salt and black pepper to the taste.
- 8 bread slices, white parts only.
- 1/2 teaspoon mustard seeds.
- 1 coriander bunch, chopped.
- 2 small yellow onions, chopped.
- 2 green chilies, chopped.
- 2 curry leaf springs.
- 1/2 teaspoon turmeric powder.

DIRECTIONS

1. Heat up a pan with 1 tsp oil, add mustard seeds, curry leaves, onions and turmeric, stir and cook for a few seconds.
2. Add mashed potatoes, pepper, salt, coriander and chilies, stir well, take off heat and cool it down.
3. Divide potatoes mix into 8 parts and shape ovals using your wet hands.
4. Wet bread slices with water, press in order to drain excess water and keep one slice in your palm.
5. Add a potato oval over bread slice and wrap it around it.
6. Repeat with the rest of the potato mix and bread.
7. Heat up your air fryer at 400 degrees F, add the rest of the oil, add bread rolls, cook them for 12 minutes.

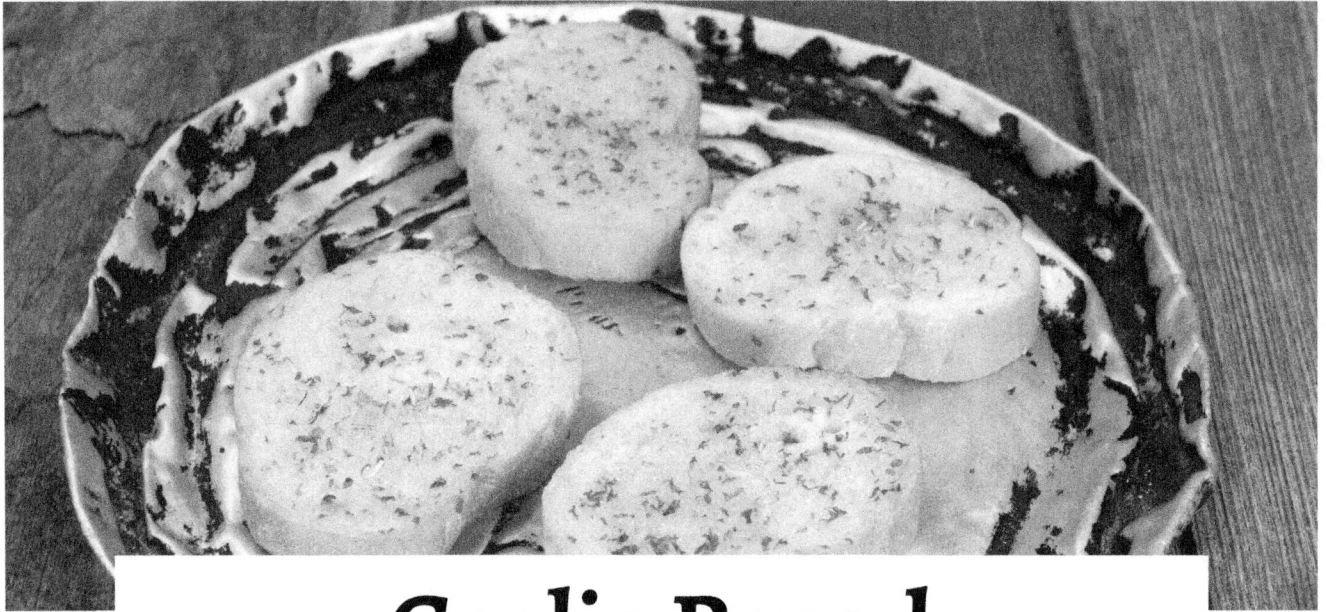

Garlic Bread

SERVINGS	TIME	DIFFICULTY
12	25 min	Medium

INGREDIENTS

- 10 tablespoons unsalted butter softened to room temperature.
- 8-10 garlic cloves minced (5-6 tablespoons).
- 1 baguette sliced into 1.25" slices.
- 1/2 teaspoon black pepper.
- 1 teaspoon salt.
- 1 teaspoon Italian seasoning..
- Shredded mozzarella option for cheesy bread.

DIRECTIONS

1. In a bowl, mix the butter, garlic, pepper, salt and Italian seasoning to combine, then spread mixture on the slices of bread.
2. Place in the air fryer in a single layer (you'll need to do several batches).
3. Cook at 350 degrees F for 5-7 minutes. Start checking at 4 minutes for doneness.
4. To make cheesy bread, once the garlic bread has cooked for 4-5 minutes, remove and top with meltable cheese. Bake for another 1-2 minutes, until the cheese is lightly browned and melted.

Bread Pudding

SERVINGS	TIME	DIFFICULTY
4	25 min	Medium

INGREDIENTS

- 1/2 pound white bread, cubed.
- 3 ounces soft butter.
- 3/4 cup milk.
- 2 teaspoons cornstarch.
- 3/4 cup water.
- 5 tablespoons honey.
- 1/2 cup apple, peeled, cored and roughly chopped.
- 2 teaspoons cinnamon powder.
- 1 teaspoon vanilla extract.
- 0.6 cup brown sugar.
- 1,3 cup flour.

DIRECTIONS

1. Mix bread with apple, milk with water, honey, cinnamon, vanilla and cornstarch and beat well in a bowl.
2. In another bowl, mix flour with sugar and butter and stir until you obtain a crumbled mixture.
3. Preheat the air fryer to 350 degrees F for 3 minutes.
4. Press half of the crumble mix on the bottom of your air fryer, add bread and apple mix, add the rest of the crumble and cook everything at 350 degrees F for 20-22 minutes.
5. Divide bread pudding on plates and serve.

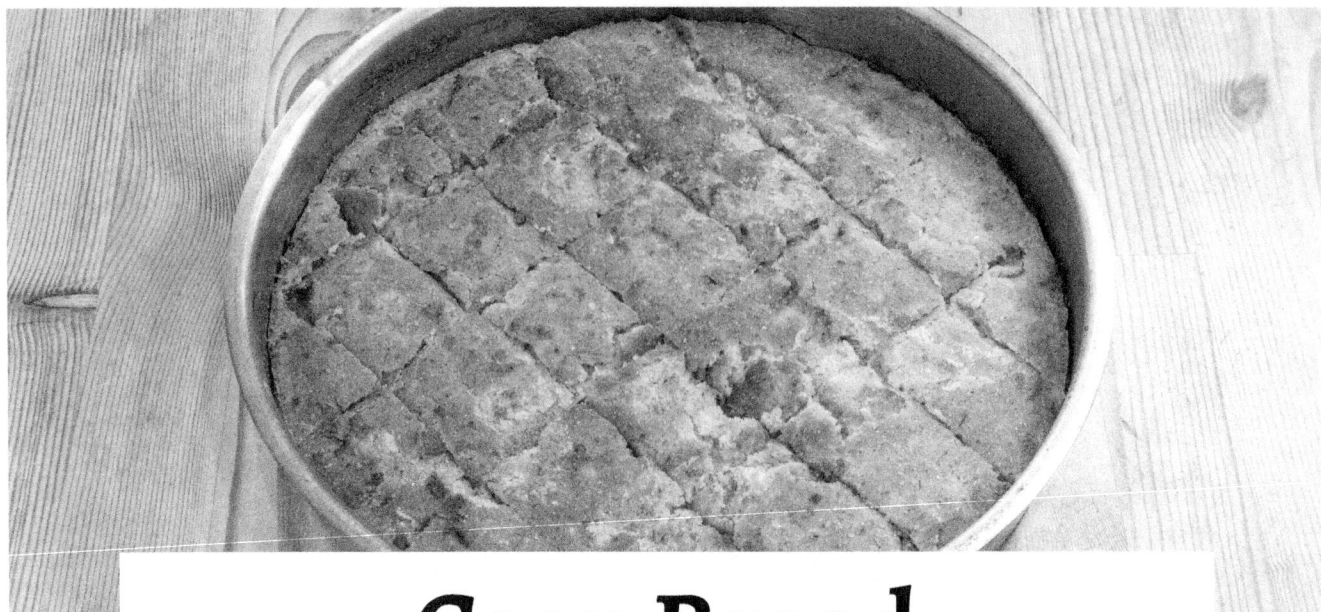

Corn Bread

SERVINGS	TIME	DIFFICULTY
4	40 min	Medium

INGREDIENTS

- 2 eggs.
- 1/2 cup all-purpose flour.
- 1/2 cup yellow cornmeal.
- 1.5 teaspoons baking powder.
- 2 tablespoons sugar.
- 1/2 cup whole milk.
- 1/2 teaspoon kosher salt.
- 1/4 cup vegetable oil.
- 1/2 cup fresh or frozen corn kernels.
- Cooking spray.

DIRECTIONS

1. Whisk all dry ingredients together in a mixing bowl. Lightly beat wet ingredients together in another bowl, then pour over the dry mix and whisk until smooth.

2. Lightly coat an oven-safe dish with non-stick spray; pour in corn bread mixture. Place the dish into the basket, then put the basket and pan into the air fryer.

3. Set temperature to 350 F degrees and set timer for 25 minutes.

4. When timer goes off, check for doneness with a toothpick. If not done, bake 5 minutes longer.

5. When cooking is complete, invert onto a plate and serve.

Orange Blossoms Bread

SERVINGS	TIME	DIFFICULTY
24 rolls	50 min	Medium

INGREDIENTS

- Rolls
- 1 large egg
- 1/2 cup (113g) water, lukewarm
- 1/2 cup (113g) orange juice, lukewarm
- 1/2 cup (113g) sour cream, at room temperature
- 1.25 teaspoons (8g) salt
- 1/3 cup (74g) granulated sugar
- 1 tablespoon orange zest (grated rind) or 1/2 teaspoon orange oil
- 4.25 cups (510g) All-Purpose Flour
- 2 teaspoons instant yeast.

Glaze
- 1 cup (113g) confectioners' sugar.
- 1.5 to 2 tablespoons orange juice.

Orange Blossoms Bread
(CONTINUE)

DIRECTIONS

1. Make the dough: measure it by gently spooning it into a cup, then sweeping off any excess.combine the ingredients in the order listed and mix until soft, smooth dough forms. Turn the dough out on a lightly floured surface ad knead it for 7 minutes, or knead in a stand mixer at medium for 5 minutes. The dough should be soft but not sticky.

2. Place the dough in a greased bowl, cover, and let rise for 1 to 1 1/2 hours; it'll be puffy.

3. Deflate the dough and turn it out onto a greased work surface. Divide it into 24 golf ball-sized pieces, about 1 3/8 ounces (39g) each. Roll the dough into balls, and place into two greased 9" round cake pans.

4. Cover the pans with lightly greased plastic wrap and allow let rise at room temperature for 1 1/2 hours, until puffy. (If desired, snip a cross in the top of each roll in a star pattern, cutting 1/2" deep, to make "petals.")

5. Toward the end of the rise, preheat the Air Fryer to 350°F. Bake the rolls for 20 to 23 minutes, or until they're a light, golden brown.

6. Remove from the oven, and Let cool in the pan for 10 minutes before transferring the rolls to a rack to finish cooling completely.

7. To make the glaze: Combine the sugar and orange juice until smooth; drizzle the glaze over the lukewarm rolls.

French Toast

with Corn Flake Crust, Blueberry Cream Cheese

SERVINGS	TIME	DIFFICULTY
4-6	20 min	Easy

INGREDIENTS

- 2 large eggs, beaten.
- 4 2-inch slices of Challah bread, preferably a few days old.
- 3 teaspoon sugar.
- 1/3 cup whole milk.
- 1/4 teaspoon ground nutmeg.
- 1/4 teaspoon salt.
- 1/4 cup fresh blueberries.
- 4 tablespoons berry-flavored whipped cream cheese.
- 1.5 cups corn flakes, crumbled.

DIRECTIONS

1. In a bowl, mix the egg, milk, sugar, nutmeg and salt.
2. Combine the blueberries and whipped cream cheese in another bowl.
3. Cut a slit into the top crust of each slice of bread. Using a spoon, stuff each piece of bread with 2 tablespoons of berry mixture.
4. Soak each slice of bread in the egg mixture until the entire slice is covered.
5. Place the corn flakes on a plate. Press each slice of bread into the corn flake, evenly coating both sides.
6. Place each slice of bread into the air fryer basket.
7. Set temperature to 400 F degrees and set time for 8 minutes.
8. Serve hot with maple syrup and butter.

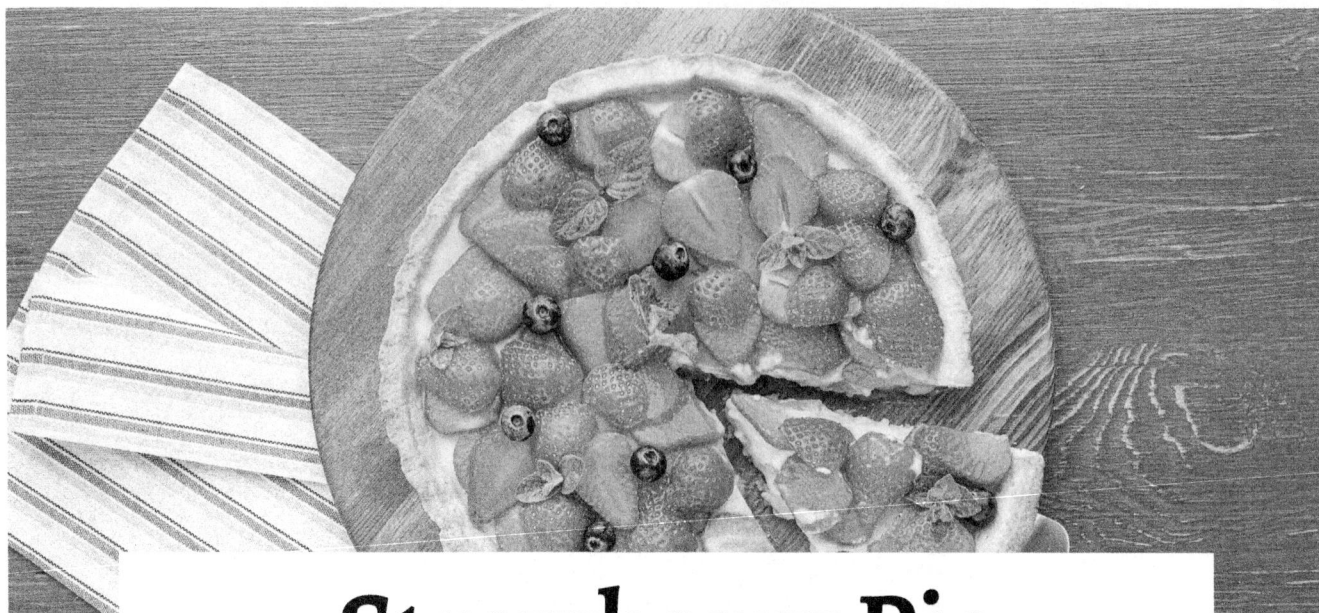

Strawberry Pie

SERVINGS	TIME	DIFFICULTY
12	30 min	Medium

INGREDIENTS

For the crust:
- 1 cup coconut, shredded.
- 1 cup sunflower seeds.
- 1/4 cup butter.

For the filling:
- 1/2 cup heavy cream.
- 1 teaspoon gelatin.
- 1/2 tablespoon lemon juice.
- 4 ounces strawberries.
- 8 ounces cream cheese.
- 2 tablespoons water.
- 1/4 teaspoon stevia.
- 8 ounces strawberries, chopped for serving.

DIRECTIONS

1. Mix sunflower seeds with coconut, a pinch of salt and butter in your food processor, pulse and press this on the bottom of a cake pan that fits your air fryer.
2. Heat up a pan with the water over medium heat, add gelatin, stir until it dissolves, leave aside to cool down, add this to your food processor, mix with 4 ounces strawberries, cream cheese, lemon juice and stevia and blend well.
3. Add heavy cream, stir well and spread this over crust.
4. Top with 8 ounces strawberries, introduce in your air fryer and cook at 330 degrees F for 15-18 minutes.
5. Keep in the fridge until serve

Pumpkin Pie

SERVINGS	TIME	DIFFICULTY
6	25 min	Medium

INGREDIENTS

- 1 tablespoon sugar.
- 2 tablespoons water.
- 1 tablespoon butter.
- 2 tablespoons flour.

For the pumpkin pie filling:
- 3.5 ounces pumpkin flesh, chopped.
- 1 egg, whisked.
- 1 teaspoon mixed spice.
- 1 tablespoon sugar.
- 1 teaspoon nutmeg.
- 3 ounces water.

DIRECTIONS

1. Put 3 ounces water in a pot, bring to a boil over medium heat, add pumpkin, egg, 1 tablespoon sugar, spice and nutmeg, stir, boil for 20 minutes, take off heat.
2. Blend the above mixture in a blender.
3. Mix flour with butter, 1 tablespoon sugar and 2 tablespoons water in a bowl and knead your dough well.
4. Grease a pie pan that fits your air fryer with butter, Put dough into the pan, fill with pumpkin pie filling, place in your air fryer's basket and bake at 360 degrees F for 15-18 minutes.
5. Slice and serve warm.

Peach Pie

SERVINGS	TIME	DIFFICULTY
4	40 min	Medium

INGREDIENTS

- 1 pie dough.
- 2 tablespoons butter, melted.
- 2.25 pounds peaches, pitted and chopped.
- 1/2 cup sugar.
- 2 tablespoons cornstarch.
- A pinch of nutmeg, ground.
- 2 tablespoons flour.
- 1 tablespoon dark rum.
- 1 tablespoon lemon juice.

DIRECTIONS

1. Mix peaches with cornstarch, sugar, flour, nutmeg, rum, lemon juice and butter in a bowl and stir well.
2. Roll pie dough into a pie pan that fits your air fryer and press well.
3. Pour and spread mixture in step 1 into pie pan, introduce in your air fryer and bake at 350 degrees F for 35 minutes.
4. Serve warm or cold.

Mini Apple Pies

SERVINGS	TIME	DIFFICULTY
3	40 min	Medium

INGREDIENTS

- 1 egg.
- 1 medium apple, peeled & diced.
- 1 tablespoon unsalted butter.
- 2.5 tablespoons granulated sugar.
- 1 teaspoon milk.
- 1/2 teaspoon ground cinnamon.
- 1/2 teaspoon ground allspice.
- 1/2 teaspoon ground nutmeg.
- 1 sheet pre-made pie dough.

DIRECTIONS

1. Mix the diced apples in the granulated sugar, butter, cinnamon, nutmeg and pepper in a saucepan, stirring, over low heat. Cook for 2 minutes and then turn off the heat.
2. Bring the pot of apple mixture to cool at room temperature for 30 minutes.
3. Cut the pie dough into two to three 5-inch circles. Add the apple filling to the center of each pie dough circle and use your finger to apply water to the outer ends. Then crimp the dough shut and cut a small slit on the top.
4. Mix together the egg and milk to make an egg wash, and brush it on the top of each pie.
5. Put the pies into the preheated air fryer, bake for 350°F in 10 minutes.
6. Remove when pies are golden brown, then let the pie cool and serve.

Roasted Kale Chips

SERVINGS	TIME	DIFFICULTY
2	20 min	Easy

INGREDIENTS

- 1 lb Sweet Potatoes.
- 2 TB Olive Oil.
- 2 Cups Cold Water.
- Salt or Seasoning Blend.

DIRECTIONS

1. Rinse kale Cut kale into approximately 2" pieces. Then rub kale with BBQ rub or seasoning of choice.
2. Toss seasoned kale with just enough oil to coat the leaves lightly.
3. Lightly salt kale to taste
4. Put seasoned kale in air fryer basket Place basket in air fryer and cook at 350°F for 5 minutes.
5. Remove the basket and flip the kale ensuring that no pieces are sticking to the basket Replace the basket in the air fryer and cook at 350° for 5 minutes and add salt to taste.

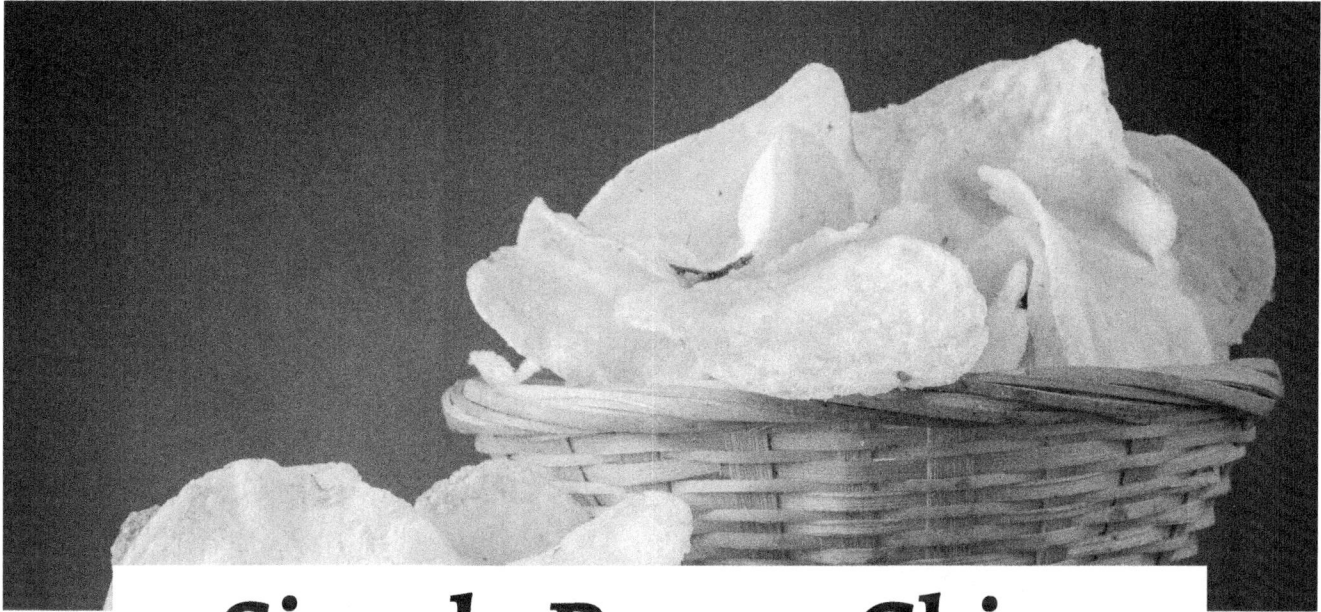

Simple Potato Chips

SERVINGS	TIME	DIFFICULTY
4	30 min	Easy

INGREDIENTS

- 4 potatoes, scrubbed, peeled into thin chips, soaked in water for 30 minutes, drained and pat dried.
- 2 teaspoons rosemary, chopped.
- 1 tablespoon olive oil.
- Salt the taste.

DIRECTIONS

1. Mix potato chips with salt and oil in a bowl.
2. Preheat the air fryer at 250 degrees F in 3 minutes.
3. Place them in your air fryer's basket and cook at 330 degrees F for 30 minutes.
4. Divide among plates, sprinkle rosemary all over and serve as a side dish.

Sweet Potato Fries

SERVINGS	TIME	DIFFICULTY
2	20 min	Easy

INGREDIENTS

- 1/2 Bunch of Young Kale Leaves.
- BBQ Rub or Seasoning of Choice.
- Salt.
- Olive Oil.

DIRECTIONS

1. Cut potatoes into 1/2 inch squared slices then put sliced potatoes into cold water. Soak 30 minutes.
2. Remove potatoes from water and pat dry. Toss potatoes with olive oil until lightly coated.
3. Sprinkle salt or seasoning blend on top of potatoes and stir to combine.
4. Put seasoned potatoes in airfryer basket ensuring that they are no more than two layers thick.
5. Put basket in airfryer and cook at 350° F for 12 minutes.
6. Stir fries to ensure that they cook evenly then fry at 350°F for 12 more minutes.

Note: *For crispier fries, cook at 390°F for10 minutes each time.*

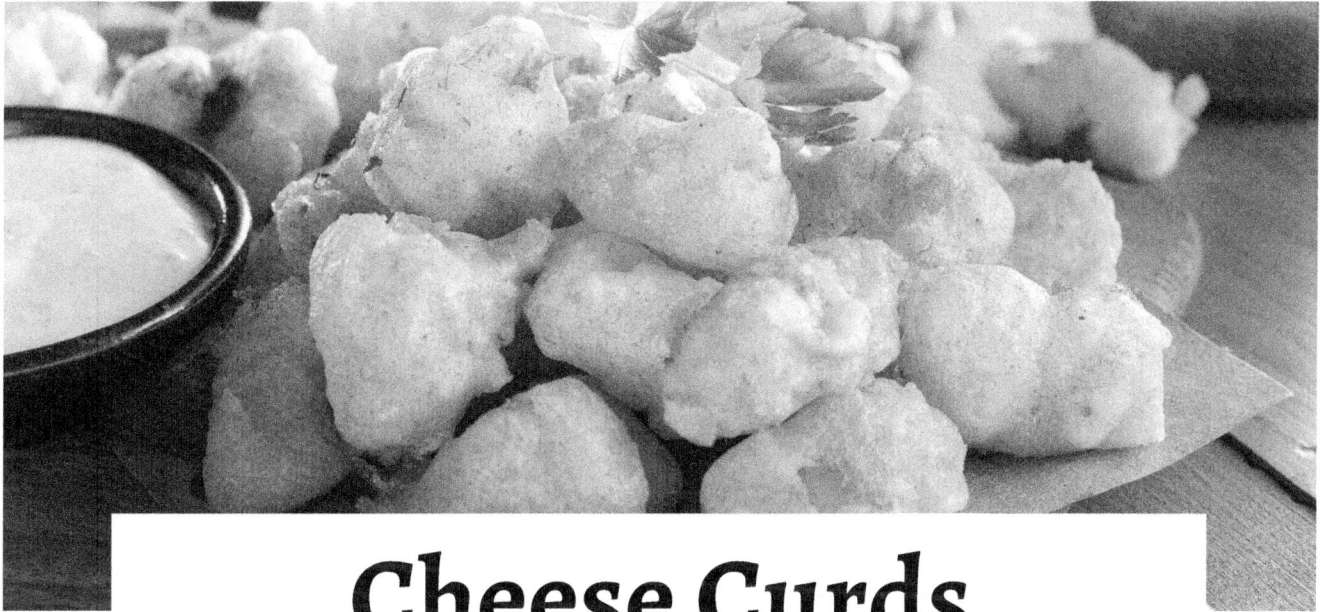

Cheese Curds

SERVINGS	TIME	DIFFICULTY
4	20 min	Easy

INGREDIENTS

- 1/4 cup flour.
- 1/2 teaspoon salt.
- 8 ounces cheddar cheese curds.
- 1/2 cup panko bread crumbs fine.
- 2 eggs beaten.
- 1/4 teaspoon black pepper.
- 1/2 teaspoon cayenne pepper.

DIRECTIONS

1. Mix the flour, salt, pepper and cayenne pepper in a bowl to combine.
2. Spray the air fryer basket with oil.
3. Dip the cheese curds in flour, then egg, then roll in panko and place in the air fryer basket.
4. Repeat until all cheese curds are coated.
5. Bake at 350° F for 4 to 6 minutes, until golden brown on outside. (Start checking them at 3 minutes to make sure they don't melt).

Crunchy Onion Rings

SERVINGS	TIME	DIFFICULTY
4	20 min	Easy

INGREDIENTS

- 1 large sweet onion, sliced very thin.
- large bowl of ice water..
- 1 cup self-rising flour.
- 1 teaspoon salt.
- 1/2 teaspoon pepper.
- 1 teaspoon paprika.
- 1/2 teaspoon garlic powder non-stick.
- cooking spray.

DIRECTIONS

1. Soak the onions in the ice water for at least 10 minutes.
2. Mix the flour with salt, pepper, paprika and garlic powder in a large bowl.
3. Remove the onions from the ice water and toss in the seasoned flour. Shake off all excess flour.
4. Place an even row of onions in the basket, do not overcrowd, and spritz with non-stick spray.
5. Put the basket and pan into the air fryer. Set temperature to 400 F degrees and the timer for 7 minutes.
6. Shake several times during the cooking process. Once cooking is complete, remove. Repeat with remaining onions.

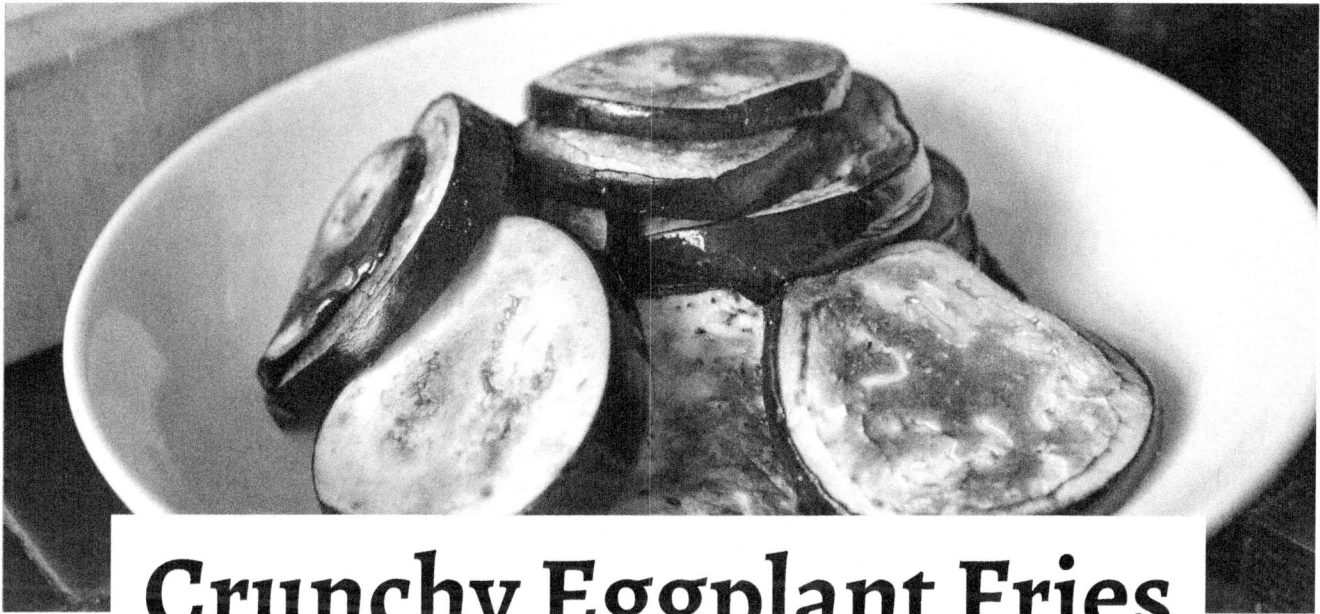

Crunchy Eggplant Fries

SERVINGS	TIME	DIFFICULTY
2	20 min	Easy

INGREDIENTS

- 1 large eggplant.
- 2 cups seasoned panko bread crumbs
- 2 tablespoons milk.
- 1 large egg, beaten.
- 1/2 cup shredded Italian cheese blend
- Cooking spray
- Marinara for dipping

DIRECTIONS

1. Peel the eggplant and slice lengthwise into 0.5-inch slices. Then cut them into quarter-inch strips. In a shallow glass, beat egg and milk together.
2. In another bowl, combine panko and cheese.
3. Dip each piece of eggplant in egg mixture then press into panko mixture, coat both sides well.
4. Place an even layer of eggplant in the basket, do not overcrowd, and spritz with non-stick spray. Put the basket and pan into the air fryer and set temperature to 400 F degrees in 5 minutes.
5. Once baking is complete, remove. Repeat with remaining eggplant.
6. Serve warm with marinara sauce for dipping.

Cinnamon Sugar Churros
with Dark Chocolate Dipping Sauce

INGREDIENTS

- 2 eggs
- 1/4 cup butter, cubed
- 1/4 tsp salt
- 1/2 cup all-purpose flour
- 1 tsp ground cinnamon
- 1/2 cup 35% heavy cream
- 1 tbsp vegetable oil
- 1/2 cup dark chocolate, finely chopped
- 2 tbsp maple syrup
- 1/4 cup granulated sugar

Servings: 4   45 minutes

DIRECTIONS

1. In saucepan set over medium heat, bring 1/2 cup water, add butter and salt to boil. Remove saucepan from heat. Using wooden spoon, add flour, stir well.

2. Continue to heat the pan on the stove, stirring constantly, for 2-4 minutes or until the mixture coats the pan with a thin film. Remove from heat; stir for about 5 minutes or until cooled slightly.

3. Beat in eggs, one at a time, beating well after each addition until pastry dough is shiny and smooth.

4. Scoop the dough into an ice cream bag with a large star tip. Using 3-inch ring mold, shape the churro. Oil drizzle on top.Then place them in the greased tray of the air fryer. Bake at 330 degrees F for 12 to 15 minutes or until golden brown.

5. Meanwhile, in a small saucepan set over medium heat, heat the cream until just beginning to boil; pour in the chocolate. Let stand for 1 minute; beat until smooth. Stir in maple syrup.

6. Stir in sugar and cinnamon. Sprinkle churros in cinnamon sugar and serve with chocolate sauce for dipping.

Cheese Crackers

SERVINGS	TIME	DIFFICULTY
15	25 min	Easy

INGREDIENTS

- 1 pound cream cheese.
- 2 tablespoons butter.
- 1/2 teaspoon vanilla extract.
- 4 tablespoons sugar.
- 2 eggs.
- 1 cup graham crackers, crumbled.

DIRECTIONS

1. Mix crackers with butter in a bowl.
2. Put crackers mix on the bottom of a lined cake pan, introduce in your air fryer and cook at 350 degrees F for 4 minutes.
3. Meanwhile, in another bowl, mix sugar with cream cheese, eggs and vanilla and whisk well.
4. Spread filling over crackers crust and bake your cheese crackers in your air fryer at 310 degrees F for 15 minutes.
5. Leave crackers in the fridge for 3 hours and serve.

Mushroom Cakes

SERVINGS	TIME	DIFFICULTY
8	20 min	Easy

INGREDIENTS

- 4 ounces mushrooms, chopped.
- 14 ounces milk.
- 1 yellow onion, chopped.
- 1 tablespoon butter.
- 1/2 teaspoon nutmeg, ground.
- 1.5 tablespoon flour.
- 2 tablespoons olive oil.
- 1 tablespoon bread crumbs.
- Salt and black pepper to the taste.

DIRECTIONS

1. Heat up a pan with the butter over medium heat, add mushrooms and onion, stir, cook for 3 minutes, add flour, stir well again and take off heat.
2. Add milk slowly to the above mixture, then add salt, pepper and nutmeg, stir and leave aside to cool down completely.
3. Mix oil with bread crumbs and whisk in a bowl.
4. Take spoonfuls of the mushroom filling, add to breadcrumbs mix, coat well, shape patties out of this mix, place them in your air fryer's basket and cook at 380 degrees F for 10 minutes.
5. Take out the cake, wait for it to cool down and enjoy.

Cauliflower Cakes

SERVINGS	TIME	DIFFICULTY
6	20 min	Easy

INGREDIENTS

- 3.5 cups cauliflower rice.
- 1/4 cup white flour.
- 2 eggs.
- Cooking spray
- 1/2 cup parmesan, grated. Salt and black pepper to the taste.

DIRECTIONS

1. Mix cauliflower rice with salt and pepper in a bowl, stir and squeeze excess water.
2. Transfer cauliflower to other bowl, add eggs, pepper, salt, flour and parmesan, stir really well and shape your cakes.
3. Grease air fryer with cooking spray, heat it up at 400 degrees, add cauliflower cakes and cook them for 10 minutes flipping them halfway.
4. Divide cauliflower cakes on plates and serve.

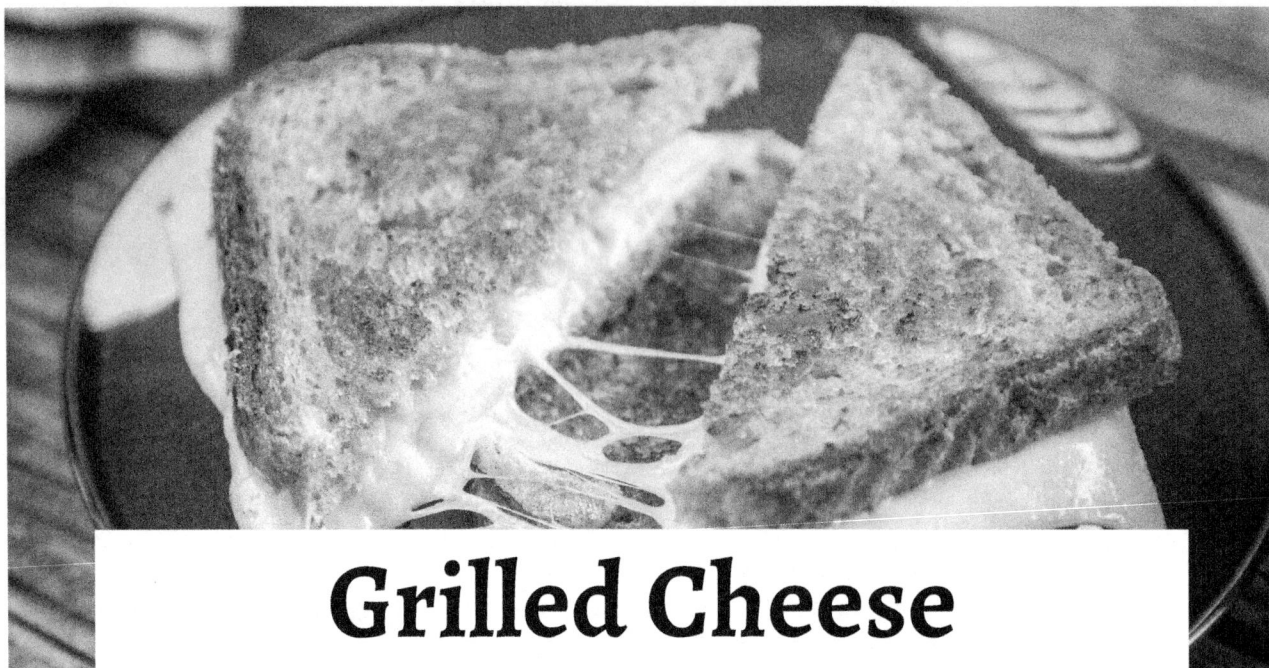

Grilled Cheese

SERVINGS	TIME	DIFFICULTY
2	15 min	Easy

INGREDIENTS

- 4 slices white bread.
- 3 tablespoons butter, melted.
- 1/2 cup sharp cheddar
- Cheese, shredded, divided

DIRECTIONS

1. Brush butter on each side of the bread slices.
2. Split the cheese evenly between 2 slices of bread and top with remaining bread slices to make 2 sandwiches.
3. Place the sandwiches into the preheated air fryer. Bake at 320°F for 5 minutes.
4. Cut diagonally and serve.

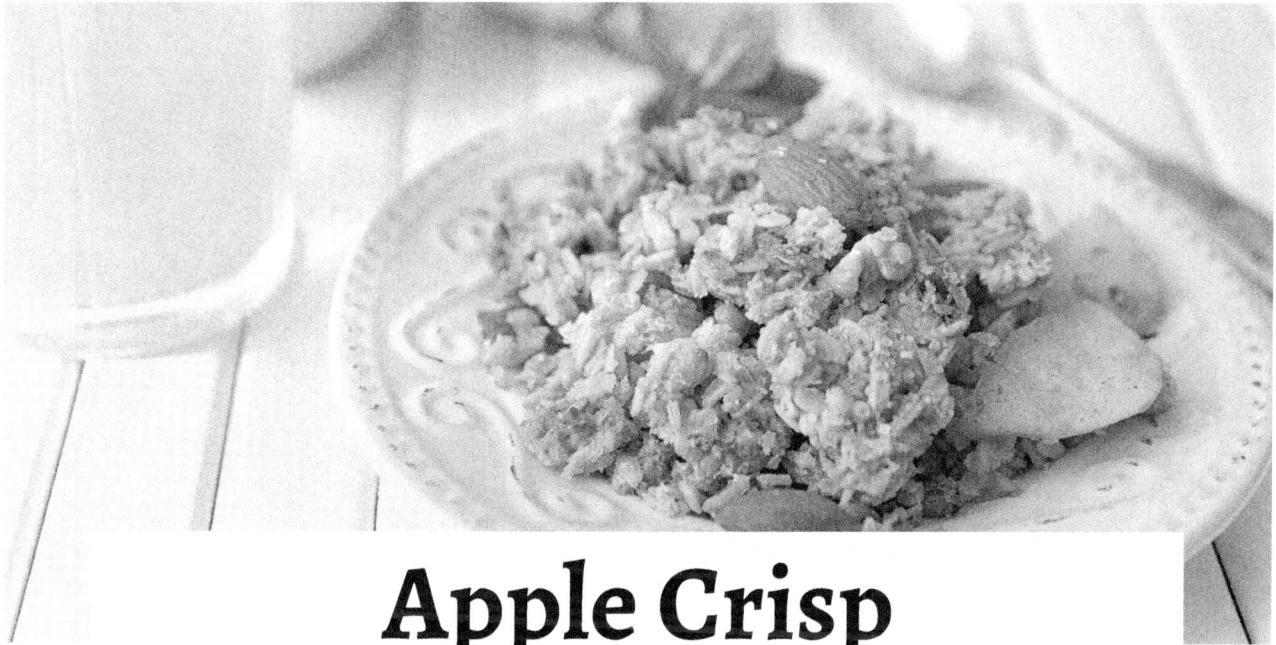

Apple Crisp

SERVINGS	TIME	DIFFICULTY
2	15 min	Easy

INGREDIENTS

- 1/4 cup all-purpose flour.
- 4 medium apples, peeled and sliced.
- 1/4 cup granulated sugar.
- 1/4 cup brown sugar.
- 1 teaspoon cinnamon.
- 1/4 teaspoon nutmeg.
- 1/4 cup quick oats.
- 1/4 cup cold butter, cubed.
- 1/2 teaspoon vanilla extract.

DIRECTIONS

1. Mix sliced apples, brown sugar, cinnamon, and nutmeg together in a bowl.
2. In another bowl, mix oats, cold butter, flour, granulated sugar, and vanilla extract until crumbly.
3. Pour the apple mixture into a greased baking tray, then top with the oat mixture.
4. Place the tray in the air fryer basket and cook at 380°F for 15-20 minutes or until the top is golden brown.
5. Serve hot with a scoop of vanilla ice cream or some caramel sauce, if desired. This air fryer deep-fried apple is a sweet and satisfying dessert that's perfect for any occasion. Enjoy!

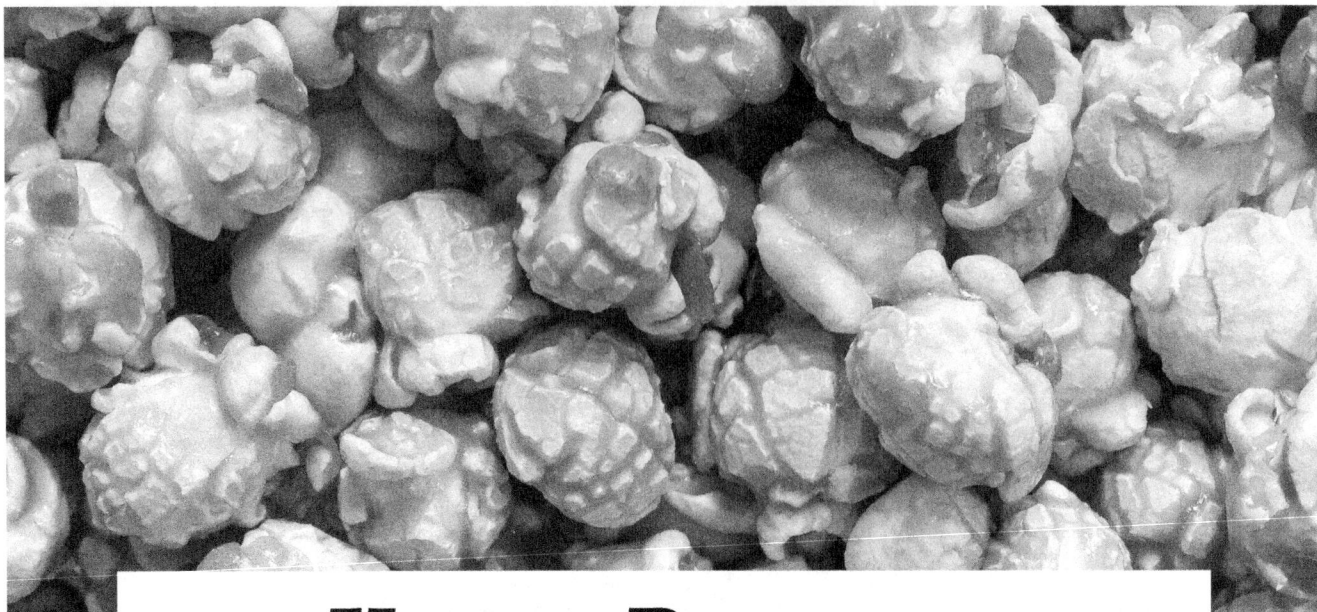

Vegan Popcorn

SERVINGS	TIME	DIFFICULTY
2	20 min	Easy

INGREDIENTS

- 1/4 cup popcorn kernels.
- 2 tbsp vegetable oil.
- Salt to taste.

DIRECTIONS

1. Mix together the popcorn kernels and vegetable oil in a small bowl.
2. Preheat the air fryer to 400°F. Pour the popcorn kernel mixture into the air fryer basket. Fry for 4-5 minutes, or until the popping slows down.
3. Remove the popcorn from the air fryer and sprinkle with salt.
4. Serve the popcorn hot and enjoy!

INGREDIENTS

- 1 cup granulated sugar.
- 1/2 cup light corn syrup.
- 1/4 cup water.
- 1/4 tsp cream of tartar.
- 1/2 tsp vanilla extract.
- Food coloring (optional).

Simple Candy

SERVINGS	TIME	DIFFICULTY
20	20 min	Easy

DIRECTIONS

1. In a medium-sized saucepan, combine the sugar, corn syrup, water, and cream of tartar. Stir the mixture until the sugar dissolves completely.
2. Bring the mixture to a boil over medium-high heat. Once it starts boiling, reduce the heat to low and let it simmer for about 8-10 minutes, be careful not to let it burn.
3. Remove the saucepan from the heat and stir in the vanilla extract and food coloring (if using).
4. Pour the hot candy mixture into a silicone candy mold or onto a silicone mat, spreading it evenly with a spatula. Let it cool for a few minutes until it becomes firm.
5. Preheat your air fryer to 300°F (150°C) in 3 minutes. Then place the candy mold or silicone mat into the air fryer basket and bake for about 3-5 minutes, or until the candy has melted and is glossy.
6. Remove the candy from the air fryer and let it cool completely. Once it's cooled, remove it from the mold or mat and break it into pieces.

INGREDIENTS

- 1 cup granulated sugar.
- 1/2 cup light corn syrup.
- 1/4 cup water.
- 1/4 tsp cream of tartar.
- 1/2 tsp strawberry extract.
- Red food coloring.
- Confectioners' sugar (for dusting).

Strawberry Candy

SERVINGS	TIME	DIFFICULTY
20	20 min	Easy

DIRECTIONS

1. In a medium-sized saucepan, combine the sugar, corn syrup, water, and cream of tartar. Stir the mixture until the sugar dissolves completely.
2. Bring the mixture to a boil over medium-high heat. Once it starts boiling, reduce the heat to low and let it simmer for about 8-10 minutes. Be careful not to let it burn.
3. Remove the saucepan from the heat and stir in the strawberry extract and red food coloring until you achieve the desired color.
4. Pour the hot candy mixture into a silicone candy mold or onto a silicone mat, spreading it evenly with a spatula. Let it cool for a few minutes until it becomes firm.
5. Preheat your air fryer to 300°F (150°C). Then place the candy mold or silicone mat into the air fryer basket and bake for about 3-5 minutes, or until the candy has melted and is glossy.
6. Remove the candy from the air fryer and let it cool completely. Serve and enjoy!

Lentils and Dates Brownies

SERVINGS	TIME	DIFFICULTY
2	15 min	Easy

INGREDIENTS

- 4 tablespoons almond butter.
- 1 banana, peeled and chopped.
- 28 ounces canned lentils, rinsed and drained.
- 12 dates.
- 1 tablespoon honey.
- 1/2 teaspoon baking soda.
- 2 tablespoons cocoa powder.

DIRECTIONS

1. Mix lentils with butter, banana, cocoa, baking soda, honey in your food processor and blend really well.
2. Add dates, pulse a few more times, pour this into a greased pan that fits your air fryer, spread evenly.
3. Introduce in the fryer at 360 degrees F and bake for 17 minutes.
4. Take brownies mix out of the oven, cut, arrange on a platter and serve.

Vanilla Brownies

SERVINGS	TIME	DIFFICULTY
8	20 min	Easy

INGREDIENTS

- 1/2 cup condensed milk.
- 1 tbsp unsalted butter (softened or melted).
- 3 tbsp vanilla essence.
- 2 tbsp water.
- 1/2 cup chopped nuts (use mixed nuts if you prefer)
- 2 cups all-purpose flour (split it up as half a cup, 2 tbsp and 1 tsp)

DIRECTIONS

1. Mix the ingredients together and beat until you get a smooth mixture.
2. Grease tin with butter, Preheat fryer to 300 degrees F for five minutes.
3. Pour batter into tin and place in preheated air fryer, bake at 300 degrees F for 5 minutes. Check that the brownies are done with a knife or toothpick and remove the tray.
4. When the macaroons have cooled, cut them and serve with a scoop of ice cream.

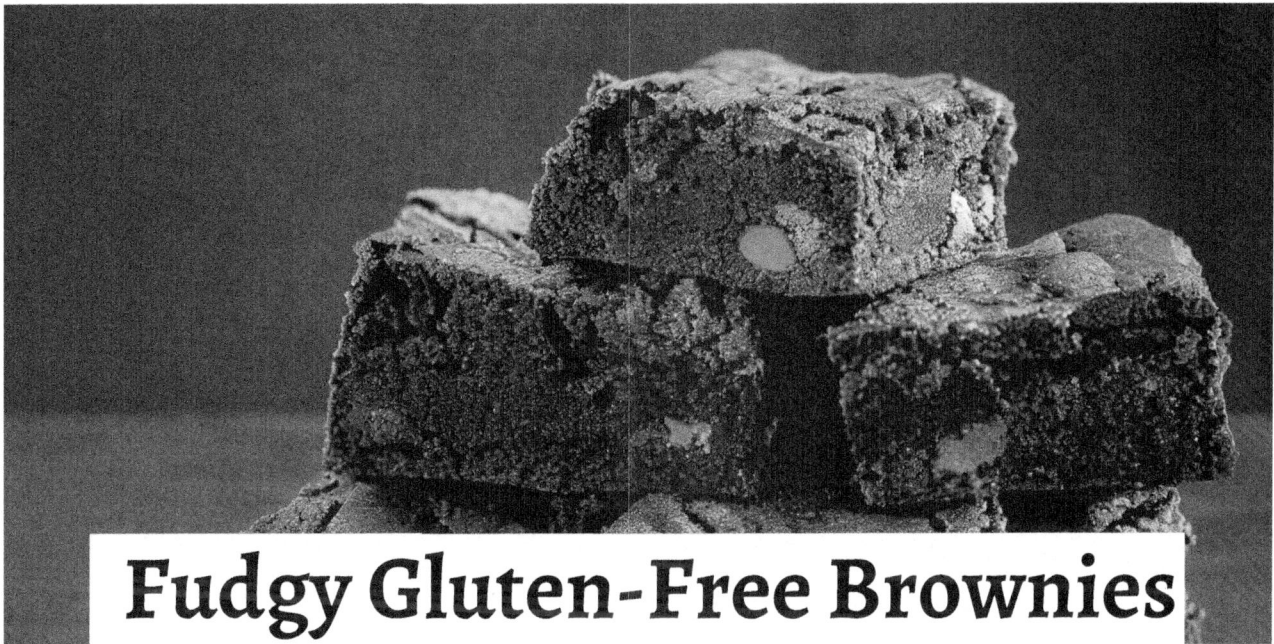

Fudgy Gluten-Free Brownies

SERVINGS	TIME	DIFFICULTY
6	45 min	Easy

INGREDIENTS

- 1 egg.
- 1 egg yolk.
- 1/2 cup almond flour.
- 1/4 tsp salt..
- 1/4 cup unsalted butter.
- 1/4 cup cocoa powder (approx)
- 1/4 tsp baking powder.
- 1/2 cup granulated sugar.
- 1.5 oz unsweetened baker's chocolate, finely chopped.
- 1/2 tsp vanilla extract.

DIRECTIONS

1. Sift together almond flour, cocoa powder, baking powder and salt in a large bowl

2. Melt the chopped chocolate and butter over medium heat, stirring occasionally. Remove from heat. Add in sugar, stir, let cool slightly. Then Stir in egg and egg yolk until well combined. Stir in vanilla. Fold in almond flour mixture until combined.

3. Pour into 6 silicone square baking cups. Place in bowl of air fryer. Cook on dual heat mode setting with air fryer in the level position for 10-15 minutes or until only a few moist crumbs adhere to toothpick when inserted into center of brownie.

4. Let cool completely. Dust with cocoa powder before serving.

Printed in Great Britain
by Amazon

21167541R00072